STORY OF NOW

For my Mum and Dad, who gave me the tools to find my story, write it, and to know its worth - my worth.

For Maryam, Aamina, Hana, Anayis, Zayd, Ali, Iman, Muhammad and all my children, I am so excited to see how your stories unfold. Never underestimate their power and importance.

In honour of those who came before me, whose stories have led to mine: Suleman, Sherbanubai, Rukiyabai, Hasham, Maanbai, Hassanali, Janmohamed, Nathibai, Rashid, Bandali, Wadimaa Bandali, Jenabai, Chowdhury and Yasmin.

And always, and most importantly, for the One.

Published in 2023 by Welbeck Children's Books

An Imprint of Welbeck Children's Limited, part of the Welbeck Publishing Group

Offices in: London - 20 Mortimer Street, London W1T 3JW & Sydney - Level 17, 207 Kent St, Sydney NSW 2000 Australia www.welbeckpublishing.com

Design and layout © 2023 Welbeck Children's Limited

Text copyright © 2023 Shelina Janmohamed
Illustration © 2023 Laura Greenan

Shelina Janmohamed and Laura Greenan have asserted their moral rights to be identified as the author and illustrator of this Work in accordance with the Copyright Designs and Patents Act 1988.

A CIP catalogue record for this book is available from the British Library.

ISBN 978 1 80338 144 2

Printed and bound by CPI Group (UK)

9 8 7 6 5 4 3 2 1

Shelina Janmohamed

STORY OF NOW

Let's talk about the British Empire

Illustrated by Laura Greenan

WELBECK

Part One
Start here

Part Two
What happened?

Part Three
The story of now

Part Four
What's next?

Part One

Start here

Watch out for these words

Colonialism – when a country takes control of other lands or regions outside of its own borders. It claims the new land for itself.

Colonisation – turning another country into a colony of your country.

Colony – a place that has been taken over by another country.

Empire – a collection of colonies

Imperialism – the goal of taking control of other countries to build yourself an empire.

Inequality – when some people lack the rights, opportunities, and fair laws of others. Inequality can be connected to things like race, nationality, sex, disability, age, class or religion. Societies can have inequality due to the history of how they were established and who had power and resources.

Racism – any belief or attitude that someone is inferior because of their skin colour, ethnicity, or race.

Raw materials – natural resources before they have been made into anything. These include things like oil, gems, precious metals, and crops.

Chapter One

Why are we talking about the British Empire?

The British Empire was the biggest empire in history. Bigger than the Roman Empire. Bigger than the Incan, Mayan, Aztec, Egyptian, Mughal, Ottoman, Malian, Mongol, Mamluk... well, you get the picture. It was REALLY BIG. Bigger than any other country, empire, kingdom, sultanate, or dynasty. Ever.

The British Empire **affected everything**. And not only did it affect everything then, it still affects so many of our lives in big and small ways today.

It's why we have some of our favourite foods, like chips and curry, for example. Or why we put on the kettle for a cup of tea. And why we use words all the time from places once part of the Empire like pyjamas, yoga and hullaballoo.

I love the word hullaballoo.

Hullabaloo – a loud fuss or commotion.

But the British Empire is also why lots of big things today are the way they are, like what it means to be British and who lives in Britain. And it affects how the world sees us.

It is the backstory of difficult issues like racism and inequality. It's the reason why we have many of our manufacturing, science, military, and technology industries. It's also why we talk about Britain and ourselves in the way we do.

But the biggest impact of the British Empire is on YOU. Who you are, your family's story, the place you live, the people you know and your ideas about the world. That might be about your own family's past, about your future. Or about your friends and neighbours.

Which means that **this is not a history book**. (Sorry, if that's what you were after). It's not about what was past, and a world long gone and forgotten. This book is the *Story of Now*. It is about **making sense of the world we live in**: who are we, what is our place in it, how did we come to be the people we are, and what does this all mean for our future?

Instead of endless lists of Kings and Queens, pages of dates, and descriptions of obscure battles, this book will introduce you to key ideas and events. It will focus on the big important questions. Questions that you might hear being asked all around you.

This also means that this book won't tell you everything ever about the British Empire. People have already written libraries full of books on the subject. Instead, we will talk about the hottest topics, so that this book becomes your starting point, with the hope that you will be inspired to carry on and do your own exploration.

This book is a conversation between you, me and children around the whole country, and around the world, so we can start learning about our own past, together. And by understanding our shared past, we can set a course for a more optimistic, more knowledge-based and respectful future together.

Chapter Two

Once upon a great big blank (which I filled in)

When I was growing up, I didn't really know anything about the British Empire. A big fat zero. But I wish I had, because the story of my life has been completely shaped by it.

I started by asking my parents, grandmother, uncles, aunts, friends... literally anyone who had a story to tell (and once you get them started, people love telling stories). Through snippets of information, photographs, and research online, I managed to piece together my story. I felt like a detective uncovering the Biggest Secret History Ever. I wondered, why has no one ever told me this before?

It's one of the reasons I wanted to write this book, so that you might be inspired to find your *own story* (see page 233). Because by knowing where you've come from, you can know truly who you are today.

When we know our own individual stories, we can share them, and that helps us to understand each other better, allowing us to compare notes about our different feelings and experiences of the past, and our ideas about it. Understanding your own story and the place you live are among *the most important things you can ever do for yourself.*

A tale of two journeys

My family were originally from Gujarat, India. They were busy minding their own business when the East India Company arrived in 1608, and when it established its rule in 1757. In 1858 India was officially named as the British Raj, or the British Empire, and Queen Victoria (who was the Queen), became Empress of India.

Towards the end of the 19th century, my great grandfather decided to leave India and travel to East Africa by boat. It might have been because between 1876 and 1878 the Great Famine took place in India, including Gujarat, which led to the deaths of ten million people. Some reports suggest the huge number was made worse by British policies that continued to send vital crops out of India to sell, along with not wanting to spend money on the welfare of Indians under their rule.

Or it might have been because around the same time, many Indians were travelling to East Africa where the British were also taking indentured labourers to build railways. Perhaps they thought they could have a better life in East Africa, which had recently come under British control.

Whatever the reason, my great grandfather made the perilous journey across the *kala pani*, the taboo black waters of the Indian Ocean to what is today called Tanzania.

One of my grandfathers worked in Aden before going to East Africa, a bustling port set in what is today's Yemen, which the British Empire established to control the sea-trade routes around Arabia.

My family were called Overseas Subjects of the British Empire. The taxes they and their communities paid and the contributions they made to Britain all played a role in how Britain became wealthy and powerful. My family had to speak English even though they were Indians living in Africa. Some of my aunts went to convent schools taught by nuns who had come all the way from England!

In the 1960s, already having been in one part of Britain (Tanganykia, now Tanzania), my mum and dad decided to come to a different part of Britain – the UK. They settled in London. And I was born here. All of which means my family has lived across three continents of the British Empire, and we've been British for more than 200 years, contributing blood, love, sweat, tears – and taxes! – to make this country what it is today.

That was my story. What's yours?

The British Empire might be tied to your story too, or those of your friends or neighbours – whether your family has lived forever in the English countryside, whether your family was part of the Windrush generation (see page 221), whether you now live in a town where mining or manufacturing were once the main industries, or whether it is something else entirely.

Maybe you can find out about your own great grandparents. You might have a story like mine, affected by famine, poverty, economic opportunity, global politics and migration. Or perhaps your families' lives changed by moving from agriculture to working in factories; by introducing new spices and foods into their cuisine, or by joining the navy for trade or war. Or your story might be about coming to Britain today.

You will almost certainly discover something that you never knew before.

Chapter Three

What is an empire?

An empire is a group of countries or peoples ruled over by a single person, government, or country. You've probably already learnt about some of them, like the Roman Empire or the Egyptians.

The very first one is thought to be the Akkadian Empire which was about 4000 years ago. Today, their capital city Akkad is in the country of Iraq.

The Akkadian Empire kicked off in 2300 BC when Sargon of Akkad decided to conquer the surrounding areas, including next door Sumeria. Legend says that Ishtar, the Akkadian goddess of war and love, had come to him and told him he had a divine mission to make Akkad bigger. Using this as a reason to expand Akkad, Sargon made it become richer and more powerful, and took over all its neighbours, which stopped them from getting stronger or attacking Akkad. Eventually the language and culture of Akkad spread into the countries that were taken into its empire.

The people that Akkad wanted to take over were most likely quite unhappy about losing their wealth, independence, language and culture. But if they resisted or tried to rebel, the Akkadians killed them. The Akkadians were probably proud of their big empire. But the people who they conquered were probably not so keen.

So what can we learn from the Akkadians about why people want an empire. And have the reasons changed since then?

Reasons to have an empire

Why do **you** think people might want to have an empire? As you read through this book, which do you think apply to the British Empire?

- Get rich
- Be powerful
- Be bigger, richer and more important than your enemies (because you're very competitive or very jealous, or maybe both!)
- Make sure your enemies can't take you over and make you part of *their* empire
- Adventure and the discovery of new places, raw materials, nature, animals, culture and people
- Because you think you are more special than everyone else and that you've been given a mission – maybe from God or your gods – to take over other countries
- To convert people to your religion
- Because you think you are better / cleverer / stronger / more human than other people so you should be in charge

Chapter Four

How do we know what we know about history?

What kind of question is that? History is history, right? It's a load of facts that start at the beginning of time and just go on and on and on and on (yawn) and on....

STOP. RIGHT. THERE.

You're now old enough to be told **the truth about history**.

Studying history isn't about memorising a set of facts. That's because history doesn't even have a settled set of facts. It's far more exciting, mysterious, and even controversial! You must be a detective to sort through all the different stories written by people in history to try to solve the mystery of what really happened.

That's because we only know history from the people who survived wars and empires, and were probably rich enough (or paid by rich people) to write about their opinions of what happened. You might have heard the phrase "history is written by the winners". Because – sorry to be gruesome – all the people who got killed couldn't write about what they think happened.

And obviously the winners are going to write good things about themselves, and bad things about the people they beat. They might not bother to mention any bad things they did themselves.

Or, it might just be a case of having different opinions because writers were on different sides. So, the winners of a battle might have thought that what they did was fantastic, and they might even have thought killing lots of people was a sign of how strong and clever they are. But for those who lost, they might think it was an awful event and believe that the other side were violent, nasty, bloodthirsty people.

And it gets even more complicated. Some stories get almost entirely ignored because they were considered unimportant. Like those of women, and children. Or in the case of the British Empire, groups like enslaved people and the working classes, to name just two of them. But they are just as important to the understanding of history as the stories of the powerful and wealthy. After all, people who make up society and who do so much of the hard work are just as important, don't you think?

Case study: Genghis Khan

The SECOND biggest empire in history was the Mongol Empire which lasted from 1206–1368. Its founder was Temijin, who changed his name to Chinggis Khan (which means "universal ruler") also known as Genghis Khan. In the countries which were taken over by Genghis Khan, he got a reputation for being very vicious and cruel. But in today's Mongolia he is seen as a hero and someone who built a strong empire.

That's why we must be really great detectives as we set out to learn about the British Empire. We have to read histories and stories from people who were in other parts of the British Empire and who have different experiences of it. That's the only way we can work out what really happened, and what we think about it.

Chapter Five

Do we really know the facts?

If you had been a child who lived a hundred years ago you would have been taught that the British Empire was so incredibly huge, and it was spread so far around the Earth that "**the sun never sets on the British Empire**." What that meant was that it stretched so far around the whole world in different time zones that somewhere in the British Empire it was always daytime. Around a hundred years ago the British Empire was at its biggest and most powerful.

A child living 100 years ago would have been part of a British Empire of 412 million people, that's nearly one quarter of the world's population at the time and around one quarter of the Earth's total land.

That's a **lot** of people and a **lot** of places.

If you think that the British Empire is faraway history, you'll be surprised to know that it only came to an end in 1997, when the island of Hong Kong was transferred to China.

I was alive before the British Empire ended. And I'm not even that old!

All of this means that the British Empire was still going within many people's lifetimes, which could include your teacher and your parents!

Quickfire quiz

Q: *When did the British Empire start?*

A: Some people consider Henry VIII's declaration of England as an "empire" when he broke away from the Pope and Catholic Europe as the start. It was a big, perhaps crazy claim he made, as England was small and isolated at the time. It might have been his aspiration, rather than the reality. Others say the first acts of imperialism were earlier, when England occupied Ireland starting in the 13th century. The truth is, there is no official start date.

Q: *So how old is Britain as a country then?*

A: It started out as England. Because there was no Britain until 1707, when an Act of Union brought England, Wales and Scotland together into the United Kingdom of Great Britain (see page 156).

Q: *When did it become an empire?*

A: The act of establishing colonies made Britain into an empire. This included the establishment of its very first colony of Jamestown in North America in 1607, or the takeover of India by the East India Company in 1757. But the official name came much later. In 1877 after feeling her title of Queen was inferior to all her

European counterparts who were emperors, Queen Victoria was named the Empress of India. It would have caused uproar if she had declared herself the Empress of England or Britain. But by cleverly making the declaration of Empress of India, Britain was now officially an empire.

Q: *Are you absolutely sure the British Empire has ended?*

A: Although the transfer of Hong Kong to China is typically seen as the end of the British Empire, some people say that there are still remnants of the Empire. While I am writing this book, Britain continues to have 14 overseas territories including the Falkland Islands, Gibraltar and Bermuda. There's also the Commonwealth, an international organisation of some of the British Empire's ex-colonies and Britain still heads that up, too. The King is still the head of state for 14 Commonwealth Realms. And controversially, some people say that it is still an informal empire because Britain maintains power, but doesn't do any of the governing.

Chapter Six

The British Empire: it's complicated

The British Empire wasn't something everyone specifically set out to do. And there wasn't just one reason why or how it grew. There wasn't just one experience of the people who established trade and colonies. And equally there wasn't just one experience of the people who were colonised.

The story of the British Empire is complicated because it goes across so much geography and time. There were so many experiences and ideas about it, that people have different views about it. Maybe, it would be better to say the *stories* of the British Empire.

But there are some big themes that keep repeating themselves. Make **money**. Have **power**. **Fight** enemies and competitors. Side with **allies**. Safeguard **self-interest**. Keep **control**. Think you are **superior** to others and therefore should be in charge.

And that's what we are going to explore: what happened in different places, in different times, the themes that joined different places and different times together, and how all of that has come together to shape the lives of so many people today in small and big ways.

What we can all definitely **agree** on is that having the Biggest Empire Ever is certainly something that goes down as important in human history. And so it's important to know the Big Things That Happened.

But what people **disagree** about is whether the things the British Empire did were good, bad or a mixture. And what, if anything, we should do about it.

Some people feel like the British Empire did a lot of good in the world by sharing Britain's language, literature, education, government systems, legal systems, and railways. And cricket: the British Empire is probably why 105 countries today play the game.

They say the British Empire improved the lives of the people who were part of it. Even if those people didn't want to be in it. But the thing that they really want is for people to have a lot of pride in the history of being British because they believe what the British Empire did was really great, and because it made Britain what it is today.

On the other hand, some people say we need to try to **think differently** about the impact of the British Empire and whether it should have taken over other people's countries, and resources. For example, they say that the British wouldn't have liked to be part of another empire. If there were such things as ancient Romans today, they might be very proud of the roads they laid out in Britain, which we still drive on. But the Britons of the time probably didn't feel very happy that more than ten percent of its population was killed fighting off the Romans. Instead, it is proud of Boudicca and other people who tried to reclaim the country's independence.

It's the same when we think about the British Empire. Because to be big, powerful, and rich, the British Empire did some pretty horrible things like slavery and massacres. And those are things that we definitely should not be proud of. Some people say that instead of pretending they didn't happen, we should be honest, and try to fix any bad things which happen today because of the bad things that were done during the Empire.

In fact, when grown-ups start discussing the British Empire, they often end up causing *a big hullabaloo* because they have such strong feelings about what has made us the country we are.

That's because the story of the British Empire isn't just the story of one country long ago that wanted to rule over as many other countries as possible. Inside it are the stories of real people, people like you and me, our families, our friends, and neighbours, who just happened to live in places around the world affected by the British Empire. We might look different from each other, eat different foods, use different words, and even have different ideas about what Britain is all about today. But something connects us – the British Empire.

Let's explore these questions together. Ready?

Part Two

What happened?

Watch out for these words

Captive market – when consumers need a product but have very little choice who to buy it from, either because it is not produced by many people, or they are forced by other rules to buy only from those people. Sellers can take advantage of captive markets by selling at high prices, even if products are essentials.

Commodity – any product that is bought or sold. The word often refers to agricultural products and raw materials central to the world's economy.

Company-state – the name given to a country that is run by a company rather than a state government.

Corporate imperialism – when businesses take over parts or all of another country for profit.

Malaria – a life-threatening disease found in tropical areas. It is carried by a parasite, spread by mosquitoes.

Migration – moving from one place to another, usually permanently. A person who migrates is called a **migrant**. A migrant that leaves a country is an **emigrant**, and the process is called **emigration**. A migrant that comes into a country is described as an **immigrant**, and the process is called **immigration**.

Pax Britannica – or "British Peace", the name given to the period between 1815 and 1914 when Britain oversaw a period of peace and stability around the world.

Chapter Seven

Ready, steady... empire!

I t's the 31st of December 1599, New Year's Eve, and the clock is slowly ticking towards midnight. When it strikes, it will change not just the year, not just the century, but it will be the start of the whole of the modern era of corporations, global trade and how we buy stuff today.

The reigning monarch Queen Elizabeth I has just granted a charter – permission - for a new company to exist, the "company of Merchants of London trading with the East Indies".

If you had £313.63 you might have been one of the 218 investors that raised £68,373 capital for this new East India Company. That's about **£7 million** today. It went on to become known as the East India Company and it was to be the biggest corporation in the world. You probably would have become extremely rich. But before you get too excited about that, remember that at that time even a skilled craftsman like a carpenter only earned around seven pence a day.

The Queen granted the charter because the state was too poor and too weak to set out on business ventures itself, but wanted to expand to new territories and increase trade. So, because it couldn't organise and pay for the ventures itself, by issuing a Royal Charter it got these new kinds of corporations to do it for them.

In return for the corporations raising the capital and taking all the risk of the ventures, the state permitted the corporations to do many things that a sovereign country normally did – like have their own armies, wage war, collect taxes, negotiate treaties, and even have their own currencies. These new corporations were a kind of hybrid **company-state**.

Earlier in the book we talked about how there wasn't really a beginning to the Empire. The reality is that it all started with a bunch of corporations that emerged and built trade and colonies around the world.

But right from the start, the relationships between businesses and the state was a difficult one. They needed each other, but had quite different motivations.

That tension between who has the power between businesses and the state, fuelled the growth of the British Empire and many of its actions and events. And the relationship between businesses and governments, and which one has the power, is still a key issue today.

Market mayhem

In return for the companies providing the capital the state didn't have, and taking risks that the state itself didn't want to take, the charter gave them a monopoly over trade in a specific geographic region. And the names of the companies usually reflected the region they focused on.

The Venetian Company traded in Italy, the Turkey Company traded spices and carpets in the eastern Mediterranean. The Muscovy Company traded with Russia.

Unfortunately, many of these corporations engaged in the worst way to make money: slavery. Either they traded enslaved people or used their labour to create products. Sadly, driven by profit motives, the corporations saw enslaved people as commodities. Things to be bought and sold, and treated like goods, rather than as people.

Those who held power in the state were also happy to be involved. The Duke of York, who went on to become King James II, had his initials branded on to enslaved people by hot irons. The Royal African Company branded "RAC" on to enslaved people they transported to the New World. The Virginia Company traded in cotton for textiles, sugar and tobacco in Virginia in the Americas. But they relied on enslaved labour to do the hard work on the plantations and keep costs low so they could make profits.

There were a LOT of corporations that were set up. And they made loads of money. That meant wealth and taxes to the government too, and extending more power for the British state around the world. This meant the state, and the leading individuals within it, were happy to encourage and support their behaviour.

Is competition healthy or unhealthy?

In the 1400s, when the Age of Discovery set in, the European countries Portugal, Spain, Holland, Italy, France, and England wanted to explore new routes around the world, for trade. The vast Mongol empire to the east (see page 23) was breaking up, so it wasn't safe for merchants or explorers to go there via land. The Ottomans in today's Turkey, and the Venetians controlled access across the Mediterranean. And when the Ottomans captured Constantinople in 1453, the Europeans had to pay heavy taxes on the luxury items from India like spices, sugar and teas which were very precious for Europeans. India, at that time, was part of the Mughal empire, which by 1700 was the richest empire in the world.

It's worth remembering that even though this period is now called the Age of Discovery (or sometimes called the Age of Exploration) there were, in fact, already people and civilisations living in all those places. Europeans only discovered them for themselves. That's why Columbus was greeted by the Taino people when he landed on today's Bahamas in 1492 when he "discovered" America.

The European countries were in competition. They all wanted to be richer and more powerful than each other and raced around the world to grab resources and land. Portugal and Spain began trading in South America, with a focus on gold and slavery. England wanted a piece of that action. And all of them wanted to find new trade routes to India, because whoever found it first would generate wealth for their nations. Which is how they set out around Africa and ended up across the Atlantic.

Corporations were a way for countries to get ahead of their competitors. So, they were given a lot of freedom to behave as they wanted, which was usually pretty badly as the case of slavery shows.

Spices were the thing that everybody wanted. If you go to your local supermarket today, you might take for granted things like cinnamon, turmeric, peppercorns nutmeg. But in the 16th century these were extremely precious and in high demand. The race was on to bring them back to Europe where there were huge profits to be made.

The Portuguese dominated the spice trade in the 16th century and eventually supplies to England were restricted. The price of pepper trebled. The English were not going to stand for expensive pepper! To get control of their own supply of pepper, the idea of the English East India company was born. What a reason to start the world's biggest corporation!

The Dutch East Indies Company beat the English East India Company in the East Indies (today known as Indonesia), which is why the latter turned its attention to India.

Rival empires

During the reign of Queen Elizabeth I, Spain was the most powerful European country in the world. There was tension between the two, with each attacking the other for supremacy. You might have heard of the Spanish Armada in 1588 when Spain attacked England. There was also piracy, jealousy and competition for enslaved people and the riches of the New World.

It's no secret that France and England (and later Britain) were at odds with each other. And this continued in the era of empire. In the fight for Africa, some areas were taken by the French, others by Britain. The same in the Middle East, of which some came under French rule and others under the British. And similarly, in Southeast Asia, often referred to with the French word "Indochine". This rivalry was particularly apparent over the control of India in the 18th century. After several years fighting, it came to a head at the Battle of Plassey in Bengal.

The troops of the East India Company won a decisive victory. They were led by Sir Robert Clive who fought the last Nawab (prince) of Bengal, Siraj ud Daulah, who was supported by the French. France left India, and only retained a presence in the region of Pondicherry, and the victory led to the establishment of the British as the biggest power in India.

When we read back on what corporations got up to, it seems like they just saw the local people who lived in the areas of resources as inferior, to be taken advantage of and that their destruction was either deserved or nothing to worry about. What was important? Should it have been to make as much money as possible?

The extraordinary case of the East India Company

The story of the East India Company is unbelievable. I'm so confident that your eyes will pop out of your head at the stories, that I bet you can't work out which of these is TRUE or FALSE. And if you think *this* is astonishing, why not go and read more about the Company and all the many other corporations.

You decide: TRUE or FALSE?

The first voyage was on a repurposed Caribbean pirate ship.

True. The *Red Dragon* set sail in February 1601. It traded with the Sultan of Aceh, in Sumatra, in today's

Indonesia. It stole from a Portuguese ship (nobody enforced laws far from home!) and it returned with 900 tonnes of spices including pepper, cinnamon and cloves and made a 300% profit. Result!

It had a small number of security officers to protect ship crews.

False. The East India Company controlled a huge private army, some say up to 200,000 soldiers across different places, twice the size of the British army! What would you think if one of today's big companies like Amazon, Google or Nike had its own military forces?

It bears great responsibility for up to ten million people who died in the 1770 Bengal Famine.

Sadly, true. The Company's policies turned it into a humanitarian catastrophe leading to one fifth of the population dying. It cared about profit, so kept taxes high, despite hunger and rising food prices. Rice was kept only for company soldiers. A case of profit over people?

King Charles II loaned the Company £324,150 because the Company was broke.

False! The Company actually lent this money to the King and used it to extract advantages, like allowing the Company to govern its own settlements, raise armed forces and even to have the entire island of St Helena. What do you think can go wrong if a company has power over the government?

The Company sent a Christmas card every year to prominent MPs and ministers.

I have no idea whether they did this or not. But they did give £1200 per year to them to influence Parliament. Some Company big bosses even used their wealth to buy Parliamentary seats to pass laws favourable to themselves or turn a blind eye to dodgy dealings. What might happen in a democracy if rich businesses and people can influence Parliament and law-making?

It ruled a country.

True! After the Battle of Plassey (1757) and the Battle of Buxar (1764), and the granting of revenue rights for tax collection, Sir Robert Clive took over the whole government in Bengal and eventually India. The Company had its own army to maintain control over the area. And civil servants to manage administration. I think you'd call that pretty much ruling a country, but do you think corporations should be running countries?

It had its own currency and coins.

True. The Company had its own mint in India, and the currency became the foundation of trade across the Empire in the east, remaining a part of Indian life until its independence in 1947. Some corporations today are creating their own digital cryptocurrencies. How do you think this might change the relationship between corporations, the government, and ordinary people if money can bypass the state?

The Indians didn't like the East India Company's rule and mounted rebellions across the country.

True! The First Indian War of Independence in 1857 led to a horrific response by the Company, with massacres and death. At home in Britain there was anger at the Company's behaviour. But also, that the government had to keep bailing the Company out and picking up the pieces when it messed up.

But Britain was enjoying being rich off the proceeds of India, so it decided to take over. In 1857, Queen Victoria was declared the Empress and in 1858 the British Raj over India began. The rule of the East India Company in India was over for good. And in 1874, just under 275 years after Queen Elizabeth I had granted the company its Royal Charter, it was dissolved forever.

People today complain that corporations do whatever they want to make profits, and the government is left to fix the things that go wrong.

Having clear, strong rules that companies have to follow right from the start seems to be the lesson to learn from the exploits of the East India Company.

Shop till you drop

If you go into a shop today, you probably don't think much of the fact that a product might be designed in London, the raw materials grown in India, the item manufactured in China, shipped to Italy for finishing, sent back to London HQ, Paris, and New York for marketing and then sold in Manchester, Glasgow, Belfast, or Cardiff, all under one brand. But it was the global corporations that first emerged in this period that paved the way for the movement of goods that we are familiar with today.

Some of those early companies still exist. For example, the Hudson's Bay Company is the world's oldest existing joint stock corporation, founded in 1670. It still has 250 department stores in Canada and the USA, including the luxury store Saks Fifth Avenue.

Whole new industries built up around the British Empire composed of a new wave of corporations. Take travel for example. P&O started providing steam liners to transport people to different parts of the Empire. Thomas Cook offered travel packages to the middle class (see page 146 for more about the class system).

When you're at the shops you can look out for chocolates by brands like Cadbury's and Fry's. Or you might not have realised that familiar tea brands like Lipton and Twinings have their roots in the British Empire.

In fact, as so many commodities burst into the marketplace, developing a brand was important. And as printed materials became more commonplace so did advertisements for those brands.

Domestic corporations also emerged at this time. These businesses started exporting around the world, using the corporations' trade networks. And their brands were tied to the idea of British superiority and quality which enhanced sales and brand reputation around the world, something that still applies today.

The corporations needed other kinds of services too. Banking and finance were central to this, and investment banks sprung up to finance the expeditions. Insurance for the voyages was important and insurance companies were founded to protect companies against the possibility of failed missions. After all, shipwrecks, attacks by competitors, piracy on the high seas, or the havoc of illness could destroy profits.

The original site of East India House – the offices of the East India Company at its height – is now home to Lloyds of London. Lloyds Coffee House of 1688 turned into a business that offered shipping insurance to traders, including slave traders. These transported millions of enslaved African people by Britain's vast shipping industry, and Lloyds was the global centre for insuring that industry. Today Lloyd's apologises for its role in the slave trade.

It shows how so much around us is intertwined with the history of the British Empire.

Consumers then, consumers now

Corporations introduced consumers to a new wide range of products, from simple basics, like cotton clothes, to the most expensive and sophisticated luxuries like silk, porcelain, and rare spices. And not only that, with more and more of these goods coming in and more and more competition, it also meant the price of them started to come down. For consumers, this was a very exciting time.

It was also a great time to be an investor. For the first time, the benefits of business could go beyond just the super wealthy or the well-connected by opening trade to ordinary people. It was an important step towards improving the distribution of wealth, and a way for people to rise out of poverty.

On the other hand, the companies they were buying from or investing in were involved in a lot of horrible activities. These included selling illegal products like the drug opium (see page 102), killing people who rebelled, and using indentured labourers and enslaved people who were living in terrible conditions.

It's easy for us to look back and wonder how people were okay about owning shares in these companies, owning enslaved people, or buying these products. But I wonder if there are similarities to our own lives today.

We enjoy easy, quick, and often fantastic consumer experiences. And we have more opportunities than ever to set up and invest in profitable businesses.

But it's also true that many products we consume or invest in today are manufactured by adults and even children, who are working in terrible conditions and for terrible pay, which might not be slavery, but is definitely exploitation (see page 73). And many resources are stolen or bought at exploitative prices, and damage is done to the environment and the climate.

Do you think children living a hundred years from now will wonder why we were okay about doing this, and why we didn't change things?

The next frontier

The world was so unknown by the European powers as they set out in the 15th, 16th and 17th centuries that they thought America was India, and were too scared to sail past the west coast of Africa because they didn't know if there was land after that.

But the Companies quickly developed new technologies and ambitions to conquer these "new" worlds. They often ignored the people already living there, or controlled their lives to gain access to their resources for themselves. They were concerned only with advancing the causes of their state, and of course to make money. It was called **corporate imperialism**.

But today almost everything has been discovered, opportunities and resources are running out, and there's a climate emergency.

What's next?

Digital space and galactic space.

The Internet is already filled with huge corporations like social media companies, retailers and search engines that spread across the world. Some of them are actually bigger, more powerful and have more money than countries. And just like the corporations of the Empire, they take over parts of the state. In modern times they provide public services online, offer the place where political discussions happen, and even trade currency there.

As we face the next frontiers, we run the risk of the same things happening again. We risk exploitation, profiting in unethical ways from others, destroying people and damaging the natural world. And what about places beyond Earth?

Some corporations are leading the way in space travel, and are working on technology that might one day mine resources from other planets. Others are developing ways to build colonies in space for people to live there.

Sounds familiar, doesn't it?

And when we go to space, how do we make sure we don't cause destruction, but instead safeguard the lifeforms, environment, and resources we find there? How do we make sure that the mistakes of the past aren't repeated in cyberspace? Especially when it comes to the balance of power between corporations and the state, and the possible terrible impacts on ordinary people.

Let's trade! The £7 million challenge

States need strong, innovative, profitable businesses, and businesses need good governance and state support. They both have a duty to be fair and ethical.

They benefit each other, but they also can conflict with each other. One thing that's loud and clear from the stories of the past is that getting the balance right is not easy.

When the first corporations emerged, the world was changing, with new technologies, new ideas and new frontiers. That description of the world feels very similar to today. Which means maybe it's also time for a totally new kind of corporation to be created as well. And we can learn lessons from the corporations of the British Empire, what they did well and the things they did wrong.

That's where you come in.

Let's imagine it's New Year's Eve and this time it's *you* that has £7 million to create a business that makes money and can transform our world (I'm assuming you'd like to transform it for the better). What kind of corporation would you create?

Or maybe, you'll say, even this isn't radical enough. Maybe we need to think of something entirely different. I wonder what it might be.

Chapter Eight

Enslaved children for sale

S lavery was commonplace, a feature of the British Empire since 1562 when Sir John Hawkins set out on the first English slaving expedition For many people, owning an enslaved person to work in your home or in your business or plantation around the world was perfectly normal. And if you beat them, tortured them or they died, then that was considered normal too.

We probably have an image in our minds of wealthy plantation owners of enslaved people. But many ordinary people across the whole of Britain also purchased enslaved people as a source of income. This included all sorts of people from local vicars, to shopkeepers and widows.

And it wasn't just adults who were enslaved. Here are some adverts that appeared in British newspapers selling children to work for others.

> To be DISPOSED OF,
>
> A HANDSOME BLACK BOY, about thirteen years of age, very well qualified for making a household servant, serving a table well etc. of a fine constitution, inured to the climate, and has had the small-pox. Any person inclining to purchase him, may call at Mr. William Reid's, iron-monger opposite the door of the city guard.

> A NY Person disposed to buy a Negro Boy or Girl; the Boy is about 14 years old, the Girl about eight, both well-proportion'd; the Boy is able to wait at a Gentleman's Table, the Girl in the House, and works with her Needle.
>
> For further Particulars, enquire of Mr. Samuel Downes, Distiller, In Deptford.

They were just like you, an eight-year-old girl, a thirteen-year-old boy, another boy who was fourteen. Enslaved children. Allowed by British law to be owned like objects. No school, no friends, no parents, no future, no freedom, and at the mercy of masters who could beat or torture them if they liked.

Over a period of 350 years, more than 3 million enslaved people were traded and exploited, along with a further 2 million indentured labourers.

Their free labour was the foundation for the wealth, trade, growth, and power of the British Empire. Their lives and labour contributed to everything from the raw materials for the Industrial Revolution (see page 143), to their forced unpaid work to produce goods like sugar, cotton and tobacco which drove the Empire's trade.

As a result, the British Empire grew very wealthy, as did many slave traders, merchants, businesspeople and in fact many ordinary people.

As we will learn later, even though many of the ordinary people and the working classes were exploited, and that they had a lot in common with those exploited in the colonies, the influx of wealth into Britain meant that overall there were benefits to overall standards of living.

And with wealth came power, technology, influence, and expansion. The legacy of that wealth is still found today in the country's current wealth, influence and level of advancement, as well as its position in the world.

But it also left other legacies. Like the movement of millions of people around the world, often against their will. The draining of people and wealth from the colonies. And the racism and inequality that exists within countries as well as between countries. **There are two stories of slavery: the story of making money and building wealth, and the story of the people who were enslaved.**

You can think of these two stories as two sides of an equation, where wealth moves from one side to the other.

Loss

for those who were enslaved

Being sold means loss of your freedom and is it possible to calculate the value of this?

Being forced to work for others for free means you can't make money for yourself to build a life for you and your family.

Individuals and families lose wealth, opportunity, and power. Being forced to work for others for free, restricted from education, rights, and respect, and forced into conditions of broken families such as parents not being able to spend time with children, they haven't been able to build wealth for their families. Today, racism can still affect your life and opportunities.

Your country loses its labour and resources, which means losing its opportunities and ability to create wealth, power, and influence, leading to a potential downward spiral into poverty and long- lasting consequences.

Gain

for those who benefitted from slavery

Individuals and families accumulate wealth and power which lasts till today.
Money from trading enslaved people, or profiting from free labour turns into family wealth, used for power and influence in the country, and more comfort and opportunities for descendants of those families living today. The innovation and wealth from the businesses, built by slave labour brings prestige that lasts.

The country gains wealth and power
both now and for investment for the future. The country improves, new technologies develop, increasing influence and the ability to make even more wealth, and gain long-term global power.

Selling human beings to make money
meant that between 1630 and 1807, Britain's slave merchants made a profit of about £12 million.

People working for you for free, means you make a bigger profit.
Enslaved people produced about 75% of exports of raw goods from the new colonies.

The long cost of slavery

On the day of abolition, every owner of an enslaved person was given compensation for the loss of their "property". The cost of this was paid for by the government of the time, and totalled £17 billion in today's money. It was only paid off in 2015. So ordinary people today were still paying it off in their lifetimes through their taxes. That includes people whose own ancestors might have been enslaved. The enslaved people did not get any of this money. In fact, they were required to work a further 45 hours per week for free for the next six years.

The name of every single one of the 46,000 individuals who owned enslaved people in the British Caribbean, Mauritius or Cape on 1st August 1834 was recorded by the Slave Compensation Commission. You can check the records for yourself in the online Encyclopaedia of British Slave-Ownership created by UCL (University College London).

There was, of course, more than a longlasting financial cost. There was a human and societal cost that shows today in the legacy of racism and inequality.

But how was slavery even a thing and how was it allowed to continue for hundreds of years?

Enslaved people were called slaves by their owners, who gave many different reasons to justify slavery. Let's look at some of the excuses that these owners used.

The work of the plantations needs to be done. Otherwise, how will we turn a profit? It's very hard work, and no one wants to do it for the wages on offer. What's the problem with slaves doing it for free?

Slaves can't be clever because they don't have white skin, so the hard work doesn't bother them.

Slaves have been used throughout history. Why should we stop now?

Slaves aren't like us and they don't feel pain in the same way.

We give them better lives. We give them food and homes AND they get to spend time with civilised, superior people like us.

Slaves are happy in slavery.

Would they be happy to be enslaved? Would you be happy if you had your freedom taken away and you were forced to work for others?

When I think about people using these reasons to justify dehumanising people for their own comfort and profits, it makes my body literally shake with anger.

Dehumanising means that you stop considering a person as a human being, or you think they are less human than you are.

Of course, the slavers themselves would be horrified if someone suggested that *they* should be enslaved and work in those conditions. Which means they considered themselves superior, and the enslaved people to be inferior.

Sadly, the racism that was used to justify slavery, continues in different ways today. Sometimes it's directed at individuals in open ways, like rude insults, or ways we don't even realise, like stopping people from having opportunities to education and jobs because wrongheaded ideas that they are inferior persist.

Some people say that the past was different, and we can't judge people by the ideas we have today. But even when slavery was taking place, people knew it was wrong and there were protests against it, as shown by the abolition movement. Either way, the legacies of slavery are still with us, so we can't pretend they aren't.

The anti-slavery movement and the campaign for abolition

Enslaved people were fighting very hard to end their slavery. There were rebellions across the colonies in the 18th and early 19th centuries, such as in Antigua (1736) and Barbados (1816). In 1831, in Jamaica, more than 20,000 rebels seized control of one part of the island. The British army took a month to crush the rebellion. At least 200 enslaved people were killed and 340 were hanged or shot afterwards.

The enslaved people in the French colony of Haiti led the way in ending slavery. They started a rebellion in 1791, and by 1803, slavery in Haiti was abolished. The country won its independence from France the following year.

On 28th August 1833 the Slavery Abolition Act was passed in the UK Parliament which meant that on

1st August 1834 slavery was – officially at least – consigned to UK history. It followed the abolition of trading enslaved people in 1807.

In Britain, quakers like George Fox had been questioning whether slavery was moral since the 1670s. They were joined by Methodists like John Wesley. From the 1760s, momentum started to grow against slavery. Granville Sharp was one of the first to campaign for the abolition of the slave trade, and was one of the founders of the idea of Freetown in today's Sierra Leone, as a home for enslaved people who had been freed. In 1783 he fought the case of the Zong slave-trading ship, where Africans were thrown overboard *alive* so that the investors could claim compensation for their "goods lost at sea".

People knew it was wrong, and as awareness of its horrors grew, so did the campaigns to end it. In 1776 the House of Commons debated that "*the slave trade is contrary to the laws of God and the rights of men.*"

This included the founding of the Society for Effecting the Abolition of the Slave Trade in 1787 which was the leading organisation. Some say that this is an example used by social movements for change today. Key people included William Wilberforce and Thomas Clarkson. And women were driving change too like Elizabeth Heyrick (see page 70) and Lucy Townsend, who established the first women's anti-slavery organisation with Mary Lloyd in 1825.

Leading voices included those who had once endured slavery themselves: Ottobah Cuguano, Mary Prince and Olaudah Equiano (see pages 74, 75 and 184) whose books made a powerful impact.

John Newton, who had been a slave trader himself but regretted it, wrote the hymn *Amazing Grace* which inspired many to join the campaign for abolition.

There were even children's books written to show kids the horrific experiences of enslaved people. *The Black Man's Lament, or, How to Make Sugar* was published by Amelia Opie in 1826 and asked children to help end slavery.

The sugar boycott

In 1791, thousands of leaflets were printed to encourage people to boycott sugar that was produced by enslaved people. Around 300,000 people carried out the boycott and sales were reduced by a third and then to a half – a dramatic change! Sales of sugar from India, where slavery was not used, increased ten times over two years. The campaign was run by a woman, Elizabeth Heyrick, who had never done anything like this before. In fact, no one had, and this is believed to be the first ever consumer boycott in the world. It was one of the most successful campaigns for the Abolitionist movement. Not only did it force producers to think about how their products were made, it also gave Abolitionists in Parliament more evidence to show that people in the country were against slavery.

Children like you can make a big difference

Children were also involved in the boycotts in the 1790s and 1820s. They were called "anti-saccharists", giving up sweets and cakes. In April 1792, Katherine Plymley of the Shropshire gentry wrote that her seven-year-old nephew, Panton, refused to have his shoes shined because he heard the polish contained sugar. His sister Jane had declared she would only eat sugar grown in the new abolitionist colony of Sierra Leone. Abolitionist campaigner Thomas Fowell Buxton, who took over from William Wilberforce as the leader of the Parliamentary campaign, said he first thought about slavery because his sister, Anna, participated in the boycotts.

Creating change

It took seventy years from the founding of the Society of the Abolition of Slavery to abolition itself. And remember, the campaign for abolition started long before the society was founded. Sometimes it can take time to change things. But what we learn is that everyone has a part to play in changing things for the better. Poets worked with politicians, who worked with enslaved people, who worked with housewives, who worked with children like you.

Slavery reinvented

Slavery was abolished in 1834, but cheap and free labour was still in demand by those who wanted to keep making profits. Slavery was illegal, so what could they do?

In the same year, "indentured servitude" was created. In return for food, clothing, and transport to the colonies where the work needed to be done, individuals – most of them from India, China, Southeast Asia and the Pacific – would sign a contract to work for an agreed number of years. Indentured labourers were recruited to work on sugar, cotton and tea plantations, and rail construction projects in British colonies in the West Indies (see *photo section*), Africa and Southeast Asia. From 1834 to the end of World War I, Britain transported about two million indentured labourers to 19 colonies including Fiji, Mauritius, Ceylon, Trinidad, Guyana, Malaysia, Uganda, Kenya, and South Africa. It was a huge migration and explains why these communities are spread across the world today.

Many of these people couldn't read the contracts they were signing, or were tricked about where they were going. They had no idea of the brutal conditions in which they would live, or that they might never be paid enough to ever return home. The children of these indentured labourers were expected to work with their parents from the time they were five years old.

Very little research has been done on the stories and lives of indentured labourers. But when we think of how human lives were stolen, and profits being made from them, we must remember them too. Indentured servitude in India ended in 1917, as a result of campaigning from Indian independence movements and new UK laws that better protected workers from this kind of exploitation.

Would you have bought things made by enslaved people?

It is easy to wonder how the people of the British Empire could have bought items made by enslaved people. But there are still forms of "modern slavery" and "slave-trafficking" today. These people aren't necessarily enslaved in the way they might have been in the past, but they are still enslaved. There are adults and children working for tiny amounts of money in unhealthy and dangerous jobs, making items that we use every day. They live in places where there are no worker's rights. We buy these products, just like people during the Empire bought products made by slavery. Will people in the future look back at us and wonder how we did that? What do you think we can do to stop modern-day slavery?

Human stories and suffering

So much of our discussion about the British Empire – even in this book – is about its wealth, power, influence and technology, and the people who did all those things. But we must remember the human beings who were the foundation of it: the people who actually did the work and created its wealth – enslaved people and indentured labourers.

The most respectful thing we can do is to listen carefully to their stories, not about the money made, the trade, or the slavers – but the people themselves.

At the age of 13, around the year 1770 in Ghana, Ottobah Cugoano was kidnapped. He said: *"I was early snatched away from my native country, with about 18 or 20 more boys and girls, as we were playing in a field."*

He was marched to the coast and imprisoned in a fort. There he found: *"Many of my miserable countrymen chained two and two, some hand-cuffed, and some with their hands tied behind ... When a vessel arrived to conduct us away to the ship, it was a most horrible scene; there was nothing to be heard but the rattling of chains, smacking of whips, and the groans and cries of our fellow-men."*

Mary Prince, born into slavery in Bermuda in 1788, was separated from her mother as child when their master decided to sell her and two of her sisters. Her mother wept as she prepared to take her "little chickens to market". Mary explains what it was like being enslaved: "*I had to stand up to my knees in the water, from four o'clock in the morning till nine. We worked through the heat of the day; the sun flaming upon our heads like fire and raising salt blisters in those parts which were not completely covered. Sick or well, it was work, work, work! If we could not keep up with the rest of the gang of slaves, we were put in the stocks, and severely flogged the next morning.*"

Mary Prince has some words for those who say that enslaved people liked living in slavery: "*I have been a slave myself. The man that says slaves be quite happy in slavery — that they don't want to be free — that man is either ignorant or a lying person. I never heard a slave say so.*"

We know these stories because Mary and Ottobah gained their freedom and published their accounts. The books went on to become key texts in the campaign for abolition. We may never know the millions of human stories lost to slavery. But by ensuring we listen carefully to the accounts that we do have, we can also think about all those millions of accounts that were never made, and ensure that those people are also respectfully remembered.

Such stories are very difficult to read, and sometimes it's hard to really understand the full horror of what happened. We might also feel helpless about what we can do, especially as slavery has been abolished and the British Empire has come to an end.

But there are things we can do, and that's the most important part of this chapter.

Should we focus on slavery or the abolition of slavery?

It's true that there was a huge campaign to end slavery, and that Britain took a leading role among the empires to do so. It did put resources into ensuring that the slave trade was stopped. But it's also true that for more than 250 years, over three million enslaved people had their lives stolen from them. We should also remember that enslaved people themselves were fighting back against slavery which also pushed Britain to end it. Indentured servitude was legal for almost one hundred years. This terrible thing happened, and it formed the foundations of Britain's wealth and power today. Both facts are important, but they don't cancel each other out.

It's in the past, so should we just move on?

It's true that we can't change the past. But the past is what has created our present. It is important that future generations hear these stories so they can ensure they are never repeated. Honouring the past is important but knowing it and learning lessons from it is the greatest thing we can do for ourselves and for people in the past.

Millions of people's lives were destroyed. They can never be brought back, nor can those people themselves be compensated. But what matters to us in *Story of Now* is that the economic, social, racial and class inequality and prejudice we see around us today is connected to the millions of lives taken by slavery.

So, while there isn't really much we can do about the past, we can understand and address the legacies of it today. Like putting an end to racism and inequality in Britain, and supporting the economic and cultural development of the places where these people were taken from, or taken to. We need to be honest that it was a terrible, *terrible* thing that happened.

I do feel awful about what happened but I can't do anything about it.

Wrong. When there is injustice and inequality in a society it affects everyone, even if we don't think it does. If we don't do anything our conscience gets numb for next time. The inequality that affects some, can spread to everyone. But most importantly, we are a society, and our values mean ensuring that everyone receives justice and equality. Creating a fair and just society is a responsibility we all share, and something we should *all* work together to achieve.

I know that sometimes we ourselves can feel deprived and we can feel we too are suffering inequality. We feel like we need support, and we don't have it in us to care for others. And I know that it can sometimes feel like people are complaining and we have our own problems. But usually, those issues of unfairness and inequality are *connected*. If we fix it for other people, we may find that it fixes our own.

It is not just up to those who are suffering to fight for their right to be treated as a human being like everyone else. Anyone at all who is a decent human being should play their part.

Spotlight on... West Africa

When the English first arrived in West Africa in the 1660s, they found a region rich in culture and resources such as gold, salt, and ivory. They created trading posts along the coast in Sierra Leone, Ghana, Gambia, and Nigeria. Slaving ports were established like Bunce Island off the coast of Sierra Leone. However, on the other side of the river, the British established Freetown in 1792, a colony for formerly enslaved Africans who had been freed from slave ships by the British navy. The Gold Coast, which includes today's Ghana and Togo, was one of the most important colonies for trade.

Chapter Nine

More! More! More!

Did you know that people in Britain drink their way through a whopping 61 billion tea bags every year? That would cover nearly 31,000 football pitches. That's a lot of tea!

But how did the "China drink" (as Samuel Pepys, described it) become considered the quintessentially British drink? So much so that some people might say that "popping the kettle on" or having "afternoon tea" are some of the most British things you can do.

The solution to this mystery lies in understanding how the British Empire was built on the trade of commodities around the world. The wealth of the Empire, in some cases, was about extracting new resources like gold, diamonds, and oil. But in some of the most notable cases it was about turning once rare and difficult-to-access goods – like tea and sugar – into items that could be mass-produced.

The great "British" cuppa

Our story starts with a once rare and luxurious product - sugar. In the 16th century it was very expensive and would only be sprinkled lightly on desserts. It was seen as a medicine that was healthy and could improve the mood. But it started to fall out of favour when people realised that it was unhealthy and bad for your teeth.

In the meantime, tea was gaining favour with the wealthy and considered something to improve health. But it tasted horrible. Then someone had the genius idea of adding sugar, which made it taste quite nice. Tea and sugar became the power couple of products, and as a result the fortunes of both were boosted.

The companies of the British Empire did what they did best – they found ways to make rare products cheaper, and began to produce sugar and tea in vast quantities, reducing their cost and bringing it to the masses. And profits for the companies and taxes for the government skyrocketed.

There was a price of course – the lives of enslaved people forced to grow them, and the damage done to natural habitats being turned into plantations

Having been cultivated at very little cost, these could be exported for profitable sale. Once the Industrial Revolution began, cotton and other commodities were sent to the factories of the Industrial Revolution, processed, and then sold around the Empire as manufactured goods, attracting high profits from captive markets within the British Empire.

During many periods of the Empire, colonies were forced to pay tax on British goods, but were also not allowed to purchase non-British goods.

Triangular trade

Triangular trade describes the flow of trade between Africa, the Americas and Europe. Enslaved people were taken from Africa to the Americas to work. The crops they produced were sent from the Americas to Europe where they were turned into manufactured goods. Europeans traded the manufactured goods, and they would use the money to buy more enslaved people. Then the cycle began all over again.

New technologies for more lucrative plantations were developed, and different areas around the world were trialled to see what crops would grow there. Some parts of the world were taken over by the Empire, and their lands were completely changed forever. This led to vast landscapes like the poppy fields in Bengal, the tea plantations in India, tobacco and coffee in East Africa, and the rubber plantations in Malaya and Indonesia to name but a few. We still feel the effects of this today, on the local ecosystem, as well as making locals dependent for their livelihoods on just those crops, which can mean poverty if the price of those crops falls, the crop fails, or they go out of fashion.

Tea had to be initially sourced from China, but as Britain's desire for a cuppa grew, the country began to run up big debts because China didn't want to buy anything from Britain. (To be honest, Britain didn't have anything interesting to sell at this stage, all the good stuff came from China. I wonder if there are any echoes of this in today's world?)

To get more tea, the East India Company, supported by the British government, came up with a two-pronged plan:

1. create a product they could sell to China that Chinese people would become addicted to. That way they could generate revenue from China with which they could then buy tea.

2. create their own supply of tea to sell in Britain, the Empire and around the world, and reduce dependence on China.

First, they decided to sell opium to China. Opium is a horrible drug, made from poppies, that is now illegal. It causes addiction and death. It was illegal at the time for the British to sell opium into China but that didn't seem to matter. The poppies were grown in India and then shipped to China (see page 139 to read about the Opium Wars and what happened).

Second, the British forced the Indian farmers to grow tea. New tea plantations were created across India. Many crops failed until the right species of teas were matched to the right locations. Soon India became a top supplier of tea, and it still has some of the world's biggest tea plantations today.

The demand for tea was so high that speedy ships called Tea Clippers were designed to reduce the transport time. The most famous of these is the *Cutty Sark* (see *photo section*). Duties on sugar imports were enough to maintain every ship in the navy.

Speed and quantity of transportation also increased when the Suez Canal in Egypt was opened in 1869 which avoided the long arduous trip all the way around Africa. Control of shipping routes was a big part of the Empire's commercial success, and so control over the Canal was another reason Britain wanted control over Egypt.

Back to our cup of tea. In the early 1800s, the 7th Duchess of Bedford and lifelong friend of Queen

Victoria, Anna Russell, decided that she was hungry in between lunch and dinner and introduced the idea of afternoon tea (with cake of course). And so, teatime was born. Workers at factories would take tea breaks at mid-morning and mid-afternoon. The hot, sugary drink gave them an energy boost. For the business owners, the sugar provided cheap calories to keep workers going. Later, the tea break became a point of argument between workers in the factories who demanded a break and employers who didn't want them to waste time on breaks when they could be working. See page 114 for more about the fight for workers' rights resulting from the Industrial Revolution.

Do you think the enslaved people on the sugar plantations, the exploited workers, or indentured labourers far away on tea plantations and the workers in the factories ever wondered about each other, how their labour was being used, and who was really making profits? They all worked in different kinds of conditions but were connected with an invisible line.

Do you think the consumers of the time thought about it?

With all this tea drinking and a rising middle class, there was a boom in the British pottery industry, with technological innovation and new industries being set up employing British workers and sending high quality British goods around the world. British consumers might well have been sipping their tea in one of a new range of teacups by companies such as Wedgewood and Royal Doulton.

When you're dunking your chocolate digestive into a cup of tea, you can think about how much history of the Empire, its enslaved peoples, plantations and working classes are dissolved inside it.

Biscuit, anyone?

The new consumer

The wealth being generated by commodities from the Empire, led to rising living standards across Britain, as well as the rise of the middle class who could afford things beyond the basic necessities of life. In fact, as people had more money, showing off the expensive things you'd bought became important if you wanted to improve your social status. In the Georgian period, that could mean anything from wearing the latest clothes or huge wigs, to showing off a banana or a pineapple. The latter could cost around £6,000 in today's money and was so desirable and rare that consumers could rent a pineapple for the night to show off to their friends.

The desire for more goods was fanned by the increasing availability of printed magazines showing off all these amazing new items, and they set consumer tastes and trends.

Some of the most well-known brands of British origin can be traced back to the Georgian and Victorian eras. Everything from the luxury store Fortnum and Mason (1707) still going today in London, to Lipton Tea (1890) to Henry Tate & Sons (1869) which went onto become the global sugar brand Tate & Lyle (1921).

We can see the seeds for today's consumerism in these eras, connected to the emergence of the middle class and urban population.

Next stop, the world!

By the 19th century and the global *Pax Britannica*, the vast spread of the British Empire meant it was easy to transport goods and to build global supply chains with easy movement and low cost. Britain's superior seafaring technology accelerated this (see page 137). The ease of free movement of commodities and of people contributed significantly to the success of the empire.

With all these commodities being traded through Britain, London became the world's busiest port in the 18th and 19th century. Wharves extended along the Thames for 11 miles, and over 60,000 ships were handled every year. Millions of pounds (at that time!) of goods such as tobacco, cotton, sugar and tea, and finer items like porcelain and silk, could be found here, as well as people from around the globe.

The Empire's secret sailors

Time is often spent talking about the corporations, investors and wealth that drove trade. But less time is spent thinking about the sailors who brought the goods to international markets. Maybe there was someone in your family involved in seafaring?

It was the unknown sailors below deck that did the arduous work of transporting millions of tons of commodities around the world. Many died at sea, others deserted at port. It was difficult work in cramped conditions, with little food, risk of disease, and in the earlier parts of the Empire, it came with high risks of shipwrecks and death.

To carry out the hardest of all the work, was a whole contingent of local sailors called lascars who were recruited, especially from Bengal, Assam, and Gujarat but also Yemen, Africa, East Asia, the Caribbean, and China. For over 400 years they served in the navy as well as on merchant ships. Without the massive power provided by the lascars it would have been impossible for the Empire to conduct global trade at the scale it did. Lascars worked as deckhands, cooks and later, when there were steamships, in engine rooms to stoke furnaces. By 1914, lascars made up 17.5% of mariners, some 51,000 men (see *photo section*). They also played a significant role in Britain's World War efforts.

Lascars were given far worse contracts than other sailors, received only one fifth of British pay and had far inferior living conditions. They were put into boiling hot engine rooms because ship owners held bizarre views that they could withstand heat better.

From the 1800s onwards, lascars started to settle in Britain, marrying British women and forming local communities you can still find in cities like Cardiff, Liverpool, Glasgow, and London's docklands.

A lascar's story

Born in Mirpur, India, in 1895, Mahomed Gama joined the British mercantile navy at the age of 18, working as a fireman on ships shovelling coal into the furnaces. The ships transported goods like spices, sugar, tea, and coffee. When World War I broke out, he served in the naval war effort and carried soldiers and military cargo, at risk of attack from German vessels while working in hot temperatures below deck.

Gama's grandson Asif Shakoor lives in London and only discovered his grandfather's story by accident when he found papers about the sailor inside a mysterious wooden box belonging to the family.

What does this mean for today's world?

Behind the story of Britain's iconic cuppa, was a significant shift in humankind's abilities to access raw materials and produce goods on a mass scale. The Companies and corporations, along with the state, established, protected, and took advantage of global trade routes and freedom of movement to generate profits and accumulate wealth.

It's true that ordinary people, from the working class through to the rising middle class were able to enjoy a wider range of opportunities and products that previously were limited in quantity and available only to the very wealthiest. And why shouldn't they enjoy them? Making sure everyone has access to things is also part of equality.

But this was at the expense of enslaved people and indentured labourers, and exploitation of workers. It was at the expense of taking other people's land, resources, wealth, and taxes.

Changing natural habitats to focus on large areas of a single crop has lasting effects today. A country might not have enough food supply for itself because the land is all dedicated to one or a handful of crops. And its economy then becomes dependent on the price of these crops, and if prices drop, or harvests fail then the impacts can be disastrous.

This also keeps in place the differences that were started by the Empire between countries where raw materials are produced (and therefore basic and poorer economies) and manufacturing and service economies where higher profit activities are conducted. And this keeps rich countries richer and poor countries poorer.

Today, the workers in those countries that produce raw materials, or manufacturing like cheap consumer goods or fast fashion can still suffer exploitation and terrible conditions, that can even lead to death to produce cheap goods.

All of this has led to environmental harm as natural habitats are cleared for farming and factories and ecosystems are being destroyed. In fact, instead of getting better, the desire for more commodities has spread and regions like the rainforests are being devastated as a result.

Spotlight on... southern Africa

Britain was keen to expand into southern Africa, attracted by the abundant natural resources. There was fierce resistance for over a century from the indigenous populations who lived there. The Xhosa Wars, from 1779 to 1879, led to the deaths of approximately 50,000 Xhosa people, with many more displaced from their own lands. The Anglo-Zulu War of 1879 resulted in significant casualties among the Zulu population. The British fought the First and Second Boer wars (1880–1881 and 1899–1902) against the Dutch-descended Boers, which included imprisoning Boer women and children and burning their homes. The discovery of gold and diamonds in South Africa led to a huge influx of mining companies and prospectors. For the locals it brought wealth and infrastructure, but also terrible working conditions, damage to the landscape and sometimes forcible loss of their land. Today those mining companies continue to exist. Eventually, the British united the regions of Cape Colony, Natal and the Boer states of Orange Free State and Transvaal. In 1910 these became the Union of South Africa. There was also resistance in the wider south African region which eventually led to their independence. This includes the countries known today as Botswana, Zambia and Zimbabwe.

The consumerism that emerged in the Georgian and Victorian eras accelerated in the 20th century. We are feeling the effects of this today.

Cheap foods, especially sugar, are leading to an obesity crisis. Oil dependency has polluted the seas and is a key source of climate change. Cheap plastic goods are creating waste in landfills and killing marine life.

The key is to find a balance. Because as we learnt from the British Empire, global trade has the potential to be a good thing, if we learn lessons from the past.

Making commodities accessible and affordable to a wide audience can be good, and in theory everyone should have a right to it not just the wealthy.

BUT.

This mustn't be done by exploiting people and places and we must be more conscious of the environment.

Paying people a fair wage, and ensuring products are environmentally friendly of course will mean products cost a bit more. But that way, people only buy what they need, and that has the benefit of reducing waste, and saving the environment.

Spotlight on... Malaya

Malaya was the name of the countries that are now called Singapore and Malaysia. Singapore was established in 1819 by Sir Stamford Raffles. The British had already taken Penang (1786) and Malacca (1795) in today's Malaysia. They had their eye not just on the trade routes to China, but resources like tin, rubber and eventually palm oil. They had begun experimenting with rubber plantations in the 19th century and by the 20th it was a huge source of money for the Empire. In the 1900s rubber was one of the most valuable goods in the world, and Britain's rubber plantations in Malaya were a big source. The rubber plantations – and later the lucrative palm oil plantations – were run by Chinese and Indian labourers who had been brought in, often in indentured servitude, especially in the early years. Palm oil is used in foods such as margarine and chocolate, for personal care and cleaning products and in biofuels. Today, production of palm oil creates massive deforestation. In Southeast Asia this is estimated at 4.3 million hectares. More than half of new palm oil plantations have caused deforestation.

Which brings us back to our great British cuppa. It's now under threat because of climate change. Our desire for commodities has ultimately impacted the environment, which means that it is harder and harder to grow tea around the world in the places it used to be grown. New locations at higher altitudes need to be found, making it even harder and more expensive to grow with smaller yields. So, the people who already earn little from cultivating it will find it even harder to earn a living.

How do you think we can create more ethical consumption now, better for the environment, better for all people involved in the supply chain, better for the countries producing goods and the consumers buying them? How should we factor in the impact on climate change, of using up all our resources and of moving goods around. How do we ensure that workers aren't exploited or work in dangerous conditions just to give us cheap clothes and toys?

Will you be one of the businesspeople of the future who can create products, services, and trade to solve these problems? Until then, you can be a consumer that takes care to buy products that give workers good conditions and a fair wage and are also kind to the environment.

Goods that changed the world

Enslaved people

You're probably wondering why enslaved people are top of the list in a section called "goods". That's because the slavery of the British Empire was a completely new kind of slavery sometimes referred to as "chattel slavery". That is to say, one person had total ownership of another, like an object.

It's true that, throughout history, slavery has existed in various forms in different cultures. These include variations in things like the conditions of servitude, their treatment, social mobility and opportunities for freedom. For example, some very notable Ottoman rulers were born "slaves".

But the chattel slavery during the British Empire that was legal, sanctioned and even encouraged by powerful people including royalty and MPs had some very specific characteristics:

• it was hereditary and forever: the status of being enslaved passed from parent to child.

• it was based on race, only applying to Africans. That is to say, it was racist, only black people were enslaved. White people were not. This was based on false ideas of superiority and inferiority, which were themselves created to justify slavery.

The brutal transatlantic trade was one of the largest and most extensive systems of slavery in history. It lasted several centuries. Up to 30% of people died during the gruesome "middle passage" forcing transportation of people from their African homes to the Americas.

Before the arrival of Europeans, slavery in West Africa was a part of the existing social structure based on factors like debt, warfare, and punishment rather than race. Slavery was generally integrated into communities, and enslaved individuals had some rights and opportunities for social mobility.

The demand for enslaved labour skyrocketed with the arrival of Europeans, including the British, who actively participated in capturing, buying and selling Africans as chattel slaves for their colonies in the Americas.

This sudden demand radically changed local societies and completely transformed trade. Coastal ports such as Ouidah and Allada, which were previously centres of trade for goods like cloth, became focused on the slave trade.

This change is important because suddenly enslaved people were top of the list of most wanted goods, and buying and selling enslaved people became almost more important than everything else. And without this huge drive to make enslaved people such desirable commodities, it is possible that none of the other goods in this chapter would have experienced the same level of growth.

But if the West African kingdoms only had a few enslaved people, how and why was there suddenly such a huge supply of them available for the British and other European powers?

The change in demand disrupted peace and stability in the region. The British employed various clever and even devious methods to get the African societies to supply more enslaved people, often causing a lot of trouble and fighting. They offered highly valued goods and commodities such as textiles, alcohol, firearms, and luxury items. And to get them, local rulers and traders had to supply enslaved people.

The British also formed alliances with powerful African rulers and local elites who benefitted from participating in the slave trade. They provided military support, political recognition, and economic advantages to them, enabling them to capture and sell more enslaved individuals.

They exploited existing tensions and conflicts among different West African groups, (see "divide and rule" on page 154). And more wars meant more enslaved people, as anyone taken as a prisoner of war could be enslaved. They would even give guns to both sides of a conflict to create more fighting.

Sometimes they even did the raids themselves, and captured people for the slave trade. They built forts and trading posts on the coast,to carry out the raids. Some of these are still standing today.

Tobacco

Sir Walter Raleigh brought tobacco to England from America and introduced it to Queen Elizabeth I and the English court. It quickly became all the rage, and smoking spread through English society. Vast tobacco plantations sprung up in the American colonies to service this new need, and enslaved peoples were brought in to cultivate the crops. It's sad to think that a product that is so harmful to health, was used to make so much profit. Entire landscapes were changed to cultivate it, and even worse, millions of enslaved people were used to grow it. Thousands of indigenous people were killed or displaced to make way for tobacco plantations, and many were also enslaved to work them. Today, sadly, many children are still involved in cultivating it and rolling it into cigarettes, harming their health and preventing them going to school, to earn money while doing this dangerous activity.

Opium

By selling this highly addictive, fatal drug into China, the British generated vast amounts of wealth

,some of which they used to buy Chinese goods that were in demand in Britain such as tea, silk, and porcelain. The British, initially through the East India Company, ensured poppies – the plants from which opium is made – were grown at vast scale in India, particularly in Bengal. This led to changing the agriculture, forcing Indians to grow poppies rather than anything else, and then taxing Indians for producing the poppies. The Empire's Opium Agency, run by the East India Company, employed 2,500 clerks in 100 offices and oversaw the production and export of opium to China.

China was in a desperate state about the millions of addicts. By 1839, 27% of the male Chinese population was addicted. But despite the Chinese emperor's pleas to Queen Victoria to stop selling the poison to them, after the Opium Wars (see page 139), China was forced to allow the British to sell the drug. Around the 1850s, opium made up more than 30% of India's exports, that's how lucrative and important it was. In 1907 China signed the Ten Years Agreement with India which meant that the trade of opium from India finally stopped in 1917.

Cotton

Cotton plantations in the West Indies were part of the triangular trade (see page 83). Additional cotton was procured from India. And when cotton supplies from America dwindled due to the American Civil War and emancipation, Britain annexed Egypt so that they could gain control over Egyptian cotton. Raw cotton was then manufactured into lucrative cloth – often in Britain which had a thriving manufacturing industry. Factories in Manchester, which was known as "Cottonopolis", exported cotton products around the Empire. You can read more about cotton on page 147.

Chocolate

The first time chocolate arrived in Britain it was mistaken for sheep poo. A Spanish shipment of cocoa beans was seized in the 16th century. The British captors thought it was sheep droppings and burned it.

Chocolate properly arrived in Britain in the 17th century and was consumed as a hot drink in parlours where only men were allowed to drink it. If you were wealthy enough you could have your own chocolate kitchen, like King Henry VIII at Hampton Court Palace. You can visit it today, but sadly there's no hot chocolate. Made from cocoa, it was one of the plantation commodities grown by enslaved people.

In the 19th century, Joseph Fry found a method to turn chocolate into a solid, and create the chocolate bars we are familiar with today. The Quakers came to lead the chocolate industry because they saw the product as an alternative to alcohol. They still struggled with the fact that a lot of cocoa was produced by enslaved people, indentured labourers, or exploited workers even in the 19th and 20th centuries. Inspired by their Quaker values, they worked to pioneer new models of employee rights in Britain. Cadbury even created a whole new village in Bourneville where workers could live in beautiful specially built houses in green environments. Chocolate companies like Fry, Cadbury, and Rowntree, along with charitable foundations they established to improve society, are still trading today. They are looking at their own history and relationship with historic slavery.

Chapter Ten

Who got the money?

If you could choose how to get rich, what would be the most exciting way possible? What about mining for diamonds, drilling for oil, growing cotton, tea and sugar, setting up a railway, carrying out trade by sea, manufacturing textiles, making ceramics, selling insurance (don't yawn, people can make a lot of money!), inventing contraptions like the telegraph, becoming an explorer and discovering new medicines... or possibly (but I hope not) just taking money from other people.

If that's how you're thinking about getting rich, then you have a much wilder imagination than I do, because when I was at school the most exciting things that kids did to make money were to sell sweets or wash cars.

What I'm hoping is that you've been thinking about all the different ways we've discovered that the British Empire became rich as it traded with, and colonised, people and places around the world.

But wealth doesn't just come out of nowhere (unless you use clever maths, and more on that in a minute). So, if the British Empire became wealthy, what we need to understand is what happened behind the scenes to bring this about.

Yeah, yeah, you're saying to me, it got rich doing things a long time ago. I'd like to be rich too. SO WHAT?

That's a GREAT QUESTION.

Here's the SO WHAT answer.

If we want to understand global and social inequality today – why certain countries around the world are wealthier, have more power and more influence; or why certain people within the country are rich – we need to understand the role that the British Empire played, and how it shaped the distribution of wealth. It wasn't the only thing that shapes today's inequalities around the world and in Britain itself. But it had a huge and very long-lasting impact, an impact that is still with us today, and probably affects all our lives in some way, big or small.

And to understand that, we must also know about how wealth works, how it is moved about and its relationship to resources, people, ideas, military, technology and trade.

Get rich quick with the British Empire

Wealth can be created in several different ways. You can dig up natural resources and sell them. You can grow commodities as we discussed from page 102, like sugar, tobacco, coffee, tea, rubber, palm oil and so on. You can use the value of your own labour (a fancy way of saying, you work and get paid for it). Or you can use the value of *other people's labour* and make a profit on it. And if you're really wily, the less you pay people, the more profit you can make. Or, as we discovered from the East India Company, you can just take over another country and collect taxes. You can generate wealth by adding value through a great invention or a clever manufacturing process. Like the telegraph, or steam engines. You can create a brand which people will pay extra for, like Thomas Cook and P&O. And you can engage in legitimate trade, making money by buying and selling goods that are legal. Illegal and dangerous goods like opium are obviously a much more dodgy way to make money.

Where it started, where it went

Let's think about where the resources and labour started in the British Empire (in the colonies, in the working classes) and then think about where the money went (to those who were already rich, and kept getting richer). And remember, the colonies, enslaved people and working classes were not being appropriately recompensed for their resources and labour. So over time, wealth moves from where it started to the centre of the British Empire. Now, keep imagining this happening over and over for hundreds of years. And the picture you start to see is how the countrie that are colonised and its people start to become poorer, and the British Empire gets richer. And BOOM! You can see how economic inequality was established.

To put it another way, people, labour, and resources were moved from the colonies, and turned into wealth for a new upcoming middle class and an increasingly wealthy elite.

This has left the old colonies depleted of resources and wealth, and left them damaged. You can see this today in the impacts on the physical landscapes, and the human trauma of having people come in, take your stuff, and treat you badly. And it has also set back their development because they were ruled by others who took their labour and their resources.

We rightly think of these impacts on the places and people that were colonised, and acknowledge that we need to know more about that.

These methods of making wealth also impacted the working classes – the creation of the poor conditions they worked in, the dismal way they were treated, including children as we see on page 192, and the exploitation of their labour. All of that ultimately entrenches a system of social class inequality.

Rich v poor

The British Empire, just like Britain, wasn't made up of just one kind of person, and there wasn't one single purpose or goal. People had their own motivations, including making money. We will learn more about different motivations later, like being a missionary, or a scientist, or educator for the Empire, on page 215.

But if making money was the goal, then the people who had most in common might surprise you. Because while the story might have been that British people were all in it together, and Empire was good for all British people, the reality on the ground was quite different.

The wealthy from Britain probably had more in common with the wealthy in the countries they took over, or the wealthy from other empires and nations like the USA or India. It's also why wealthy businesspeople, like princes and nawabs from the colonies, did deals with the British to protect their own wealth and position rather than safeguard the people of their countries.

The working classes in Britain probably had more in common with the people in the colonies, the enslaved people and indentured labourers. But they were pitted against each other. The working classes were encouraged to think of enslaved and colonised people in racist ways, as inferior. Some reports suggest that those working for the abolition of slavery were even criticised, saying that they should have been focusing on supporting the working classes in Britain. But of course, we know it shouldn't be one or the other, but rights for all, and by improving the rights for one group (enslaved people), it raises the bar and treatment for another group (the working class). At the end of the day, all were working to generate wealth for others, while their own conditions typically remained miserable. Which feels a bit like the strategy the British Empire used of "divide and rule" in the colonies (see page 154).

In fact, there were worries by the wealthy classes at the time that if working class people realised that they were being treated badly, and that they should in fact be protesting, there would be trouble.

One historian said, *"When the upper classes see how such injustice to labour, even in a distant colony, is resented by the working men of England, they will be careful how they trifle with similar interests at home."* Another philosopher reminded British working people that those ruling India were the same people who displayed "hard indifference" and "haughty neglect" towards them at home.

But by making the working classes feel invested in the stories of the "greatness" of the British Empire, while, at the same time, encouraging feelings of racism and snobbery against people in the colonies, it seemed easier to encourage the working classes to overlook their own exploitation. And it was also easier to encourage the working classes to resent focus and resources being placed on freeing enslaved people and colonies by making them think attention was being taken away from them. Instead of realising that the two forms of exploitation were connected, and solidarity would be a better way to solve their own problems.

And this is how social class inequality was entrenched in Britain, by focusing on the stories of wealth and power of the country, rather than the exploitation and terrible conditions of work and how that made other people rich.

Strikes: the story of the match girls

Match girls started work around thirteen years old. They made matches by dipping the ends of the sticks into a toxic chemical called red phosphorus. This chemical was poisonous so many girls developed "phossy jaw". The result was the jaw deteriorating, collecting pus and possibly the victim dying from cancer.

The work involved 12–14 hours in hot, unventilated rooms. If they talked or sat down, they could be fined, or even fired. Sometimes they got no pay at all as a result, or they would be beaten.

On July 5th in 1888, around 1,400 match girls walked out of Bryant and May's match factory in East London to protest the low pay and poor working conditions, after one worker was unfairly dismissed. An article called "White Slavery" appeared in one newspaper which created a public outcry about the terrible conditions. After 16 days of striking, the company offered better conditions.

Another newspaper called *The Star* reported: "*The victory of the girls... is complete. It was won without preparation - without organisation - without funds. It is a turning point in the history of our industrial development*" (see *photo section*).

A year later the Great Dock Strike took place. Many of the dockers were family members of the match girls, and may have been inspired by the strike. These two strikes sparked the growth of the labour movement, and today's Labour Party.

It just goes to show what young people can achieve.

The match girl strikes were part of a bigger labour movement which featured protests, strikes, trade unions and the demand for rights in the workplace. Side by side with this were protests for people to have the vote. In the 19th century, only men over 30 who owned property were allowed to vote.

Skilled workers had historically been part of a guild, which regulated their conditions as well as their pay. But as the country went through the Industrial Revolution, and more people became workers – selling their labour in return for money – they united to demand better treatment and rights. A group coming together like this was called a "trade union". This is a group of working people joining together for better pay, working conditions and safer workplaces. Trade unions were, in fact, illegal till 1871. The business owners and government didn't like workers demanding their rights together. We still see protests and strikes today.

Money makes more money

Remember our friends at the East India Company, the world's first and largest corporation, that dominated global wealth, ran a country, and had its own army? Well, working for them was a great way to get wealthy, because one of the things you were allowed to do was your own trade. BUT, to be employed by them for the first two hundred years or so, you had to be recommended by one of the directors. You already had to have connections, and connections were usually through being part of wealthy, elite families. And only men worked there (apart from female housekeepers). So if you were poor, female or working class, this opportunity wouldn't be open to you.

On top of that, YOU had to pay THEM to give you a job. A new junior employee had to give a bond to guarantee their good behaviour of £500 (that's about £36,000 in today's money). And there was still no salary! The probationary period of three to five years was completely unpaid.

How to magic money out of thin air!

The East India Company first landed in India in 1608 and set up trading networks. It took charge of Bengal in 1757 and started taking over the Indian subcontinent. Its plan was simple.

1. Take control of the area and force the locals to pay you taxes because you are in charge. KER-CHING!

2. Use the taxes you've collected (for free) to "buy" goods from the locals, which means

you're getting them at a discount or for free. KER-CHING! KER-CHING!

3. Export the goods which you "bought" using the taxes you got for free, and sell them in other places around the world for a huge profit. KER-CHING! KER-CHING! KER-CHING!

Later in the 19th century, when India came under the rule of the British Raj, India was allowed to ship their own goods to sell around the world. BUT they couldn't get the money themselves. If anyone wanted to buy Indian goods, they had to give gold and silver to London, who would then issue Council Bills to pay India. This was a form of currency issued only by the British Crown. A bit like a cheque or special banknote just for India. The Council Bills would then be given by Indians at the local colonial office in return for rupees (probably the same rupees they had just paid to the British in taxes). This means that India produced all the goods but only got paper in return, and Britain produced nothing but got all the wealth. Britain then declared that India was broke.

Estimates today say that Britain got at least £9.2 trillion from India in this way.

The stories about who made the wealth

We learn a lot about the great adventurers, businessmen and army leaders, and the "man on the ground" that expanded the Empire. But behind all of these people are those who generated the wealth, the ones who the raw resources belonged to, and the people who actually did the work. If we talk of the great industrialists of the Industrial Revolution, then we ought to acknowledge that it was the working classes that made it happen, through backbreaking work in terrible conditions. Or the brutal lives endured by enslaved people and those who were colonised, often with little or no credit.

Now that those industries have all gone, the contributions of these groups are not acknowledged.

And just like the forced labour of enslaved people was used to build wealth but not acknowledged, so is the contribution of the working class forgotten.

They put in the hard work, but who got the profits?

But it wasn't all just about elites and hierarchy. For some working class people, the British Empire was an opportunity for them to rise through the social classes which would have been impossible if they stayed in Britain.

On page 149 you can read all about the Indian railways. Only British people were allowed to work in managerial positions and were paid handsomely for it. That was an incredible way for working-class people to get rich, and who would begrudge them escaping poverty? As we read on page 126, many people lived in extreme poverty and deprivation, and they travelled abroad and to the colonies to make better lives.

And some of the opposite stories are true too, where the wealthy and elites of the colonies themselves made a lot of money through businesses and alliances with the British, their acts often being considered going against the interests of their own country's people. For example, there were some Indian businesspeople who were opposed to Indians wanting independence because they would lose out on lucrative business!

And for some, being the intermediaries between the British and the locals was a way to get wealthy and have some power. In East Africa, a hierarchy was created by the British based on race: white British people were superior, then Indians, and finally local Africans. My mum told me that where her family grew up, the British lived in a separate area, and no one was allowed to visit. But some people from the communities with Indian heritage saw themselves as superior to those with black skin and they perpetuated the racism and exploitation.

Spotlight on... East Africa

The British East Africa Company (1888) led the colonisation of this region. The East African Railway (1901) ran from the port of Mombasa to the African interior to transport goods such as coffee, cotton and tea (see *photo section*). Many locals and Indian workers worked on it. They faced wild animals, disease and understandable resistance from locals whose homes were forcibly removed from its path. British East Africa included Kenya, Uganda, Zanzibar, the Seychelles, Mauritius, and parts of Somalia and Tanganyika (today's Tanzania).

Fast forward to today

If you've heard about "developed" and "developing" nations, you'll now start to see how this difference in development happened. Sometimes they are referred to as the Global North and the Global South.

If we think about addressing climate change globally, part of the challenge comes from countries at different stages of wealth, resources, and inequality, often because of having been colonised. Their resources are depleted, so they have less wealth to invest in climate-friendly technologies. But also, while Britain got all its polluting manufacturing out of the way centuries ago, they are still going through their industrial phase. Is it fair to penalise them now? There is now a discussion about whether compensation should be paid by the countries that already industrialised and produced damage to the environment, to the poorer countries suffering its effects.

We can ask similar questions about ongoing social inequality in Britain too. Those industries that gave jobs to the working class have in many cases closed. They've moved to other countries. Or they are just not needed anymore. But immigrants from the colonies of the Empire are blamed for the loss of jobs.

But perhaps the saddest part of all is the division created by seeing those who were exploited in the Empire, and those who were exploited in Britain as "them and us" rather than both groups seeing wealth transferred from them to the wealthy.

Maybe a better way would be to learn the lessons from the Empire about ways that wealth CAN be generated that benefits everyone. Ways that are ethical. Ways that mean everyone is treated fairly and their resources and labour are valued correctly. And ways that create a more equal society and a more equal world.

If I'm thinking about how I'd like to get rich, I'd definitely want to be rich in a way that others could be too, to their benefit, not at their expense.

Wouldn't you?

Chapter Eleven

Migration

People talk about migration *a lot*. It's a subject that seems to be all over the newspapers, on TV and even in conversations around us. It's perfectly normal to move home to get a change of scenery, a job, a bigger or different house. But migration, and particularly immigration, seems a topic that people get very heated about.

You might see news headlines saying Britain has too many migrants and shouldn't have any more.

They forget that many British people have ancestors who were once migrants themselves.

Other headlines point out that migrants from all sorts of places and heritages, contributed to the Empire and therefore helped to build the country Britain is today. Those people should celebrate their cultures if they want to.

Either way, migration happened. FACT.

The British Empire caused the greatest migrations of people around the world ever. ALSO FACT.

There is no part of Britain today unaffected by migration and the British Empire in some way. YET ANOTHER FACT.

So, the debate about migration is really a debate about how we see ourselves as a country, who lives here and who is really considered British.

People on the move

Migration was not the same for everyone. That affects the way we talk about the subject.

Some kinds of migration were **voluntary**, for reasons of adventure, freedom, and opportunity. The wealthy and ruling classes migrated to govern new colonies, and would likely have had very good lives. The poor migrated to escape the desperate poverty they faced in Britain. Missionaries migrated to convert people in other parts of the British Empire to Christianity. The Windrush Generation (see page 221) was invited to come to Britain to rebuild the country after World War II. But they were often made to feel unwelcome. They were British subjects, and had been for more than a hundred years, so why were they not treated as British?

Some migrations were *forced,* such as the horrific enslavement of people from Africa. When India was partitioned (see page 164), millions were killed while being forced to move to a new country. Some people were considered troublemakers or criminals, and they were sent away to the colonies, called "transportation."

Others were a *mixture of the two*. The Irish Potato Famine led to the migration of hundreds of thousands from Ireland to the USA because they simply didn't have enough to eat.

The process of enclosure (see below) was a factor in the movement of people from the countryside to the growing cities. Enclosure meant they could no longer survive from their land, and in need of livelihoods, they went to the factories to earn money from their labour. The work here was extremely hard, and the housing and conditions often squalid and dangerous.

These migrations are why so many people around the world have connections to Britain, and why British people are connected to others around the world. Such historic and family relationships enhance Britain's trade, influence, and power in the world today.

What was enclosure?

Enclosure was the process of removing land from public use and giving it to wealthy landowners, who were then able to graze more animals. Over the centuries, more and more land was given to the landowners through the laws of enclosure, so they could benefit from new agricultural techniques. But commoners had less grazing for their animals. More enclosure laws in the 18th and 19th centuries, forced people to give up this lifestyle and seek factory work.

What was it like to be a migrant?

Imagine you're a twelve-year-old girl called Florence, living at the turn of the 20th century. Your mum works all the time, but you're stuck in poverty, with no way out. She's very worried about your future. A man from a charity comes to visit. He can give you an education, food, and hope of a better life. Mum is pleased, but... you'll be sent to Canada. She reluctantly agrees because she wants you to escape from poverty. Both of you cry and cry because when you board the ship to Canada – on your own – you will never see each other again.

You live with your new Canadian foster family. Other children won't play with you. You're not allowed to talk about your feelings, despite being lonely. People are very hostile and tell you that you're not as good as they are. Sometimes you see other "home children" like you, some separated from their brothers and sisters. Some are as young as four years old. Some are beaten by their foster families and must work instead of going to school.

Florence says, *"I never played with the other kids, we were just home kids, you weren't supposed to have any*

The arrival of
the *Empire
Windrush* (see
page 221).

▲ Two photos of the statue of Edward Colston (see page 177) – one showing it after it was extracted from the water, covered in grafitti, and one showing how it looked before it was removed.

▶ Members of the Matchmakers Union, also known as match girls, c. 1880s (see page 114)

▶ An engraving of Olaudah Equiano, leading abolitionist and author of "*An Interesting Narrative of Olaudah Equiano*", published c. 1789 (see page 183)

Daniel Orme; Gustavas Vassa; after W. Denton, via Wikimedia Commons

GRANGER - Historical Picture Archive / Alamy Stock Photo

▲ Workers laying railway tracks in British East Africa, c.1905 (see page 121)

Child migrants on their way to Australia, c. 1940s
(see page 128 for more on Home Children)

Men from an Indian cavalry unit, in Palestine during World War 1. c. 1914 (see page 219).

▶ Three lascars aboard a ship called *Viceroy of India*, c.1930s (see page 90)

▲ *Cutty Sark*, a famous tea clipper, in full sail (see page 85)

"*The East offering its riches to Britannia*" is a ceiling mural by Spiridione Roma that was commissioned by the East India Company in 1778 (see page 37). The people of the colonies are depicted as offering their most precious commodities, as if they are bestowing gifts. Britain is depicted as powerful and superior.

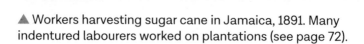

The Print Collector / Alamy Stock Photo

▲ Workers harvesting sugar cane in Jamaica, 1891. Many indentured labourers worked on plantations (see page 72).

SocialHistoryImages / Alamy Stock Photo

▲ A Welsh boy in a pit shaft, c. 1900 (see page 192). He is dragging a sled filled with coal through a narrow passage. By 1900, this task was done by boys over the age of 10.

feelings. You weren't considered as good as the rest of the kids, because you have no home and no parents of your own. You don't know what this does to you. I have never gotten over it... as a home child, you have no say in anything."

Home children were told their background was something to be ashamed of, and many of them never told anyone what had happened to them. Other children suffered horribly, being forced to work from a young age, and abused by the families they stayed with. It's sad to think that Florence was probably one of the luckier ones.

Florence was likely one of 150,000 children who, from the 1860s to the middle of the 20th century, were sent to different parts of the British Empire as part of a child emigration plan, to improve their lives, to stop the streets of the UK being overrun by "waifs, strays and orphans" and sometimes to work (see *photo section*).

Some people in the colonised countries saw the migrants negatively and were hostile to them. They felt the "home children" were different, not like them. And shouldn't be part of their new country. But migration isn't something shameful, it's just one part of who we are. Plus imagine how awful the children felt when people were hostile to them.

Imagine how awful you'd feel being treated worse than everyone else just for being a migrant *AND* not being allowed to talk about your experiences.

Today Britain has so many people with so many kinds of migrant experiences. What advice do you think Florence would give us?

Spotlight on... Canada

After the Seven Years' War ended in 1763 and with the ongoing rivalry between Britain and France, Britain took the French colony of New France which included Quebec. This eventually turned into the Dominion of Canada, and Canadian independence in 1931. Unfortunately, Canada's indigenous people were often forced to give up their lands. Their children were taken away and put into schools to "civilise" them. Canada was a key ally of Britain in the World Wars and sent troops and resources.

What about the people already there?

Imagine a group of migrants from Britain arrive where you live (possibly with guns!). How would you feel if:

- they bring diseases like smallpox or flu and 95% of the people you know die from it?
- soldiers take over your area and then make you pay taxes?
- the British help you defeat your enemy and in return you must accept British Empire control?
- you give them food so they don't starve, but then they take over your land?

All of these happened. New people came to take their resources, treated them badly *and* they had to work for them.

A tale of two immigrants

Lacchi was an Indian nanny who, in 1935, spent a year with an English family called the Marshalls. In the summer, Lacchi stayed at their home in Surrey, looking after their four children. She then accompanied Mrs Marshall on the ship to Calcutta to look after the children on the journey back to their home in India.

On the ship, Mrs Marshall slept in first class. Lacchi slept on the deck. In England, Lacchi was looked down on as an immigrant, and treated as an outsider. In India, the Marshalls – immigrants to India – had servants and would have lived very comfortable lives as part of the ruling class.

Despite both being part of the British Empire, and travelling on the same journey together, their experiences and status as migrants were dramatically different.

Migration of more than just people

As people migrated, so did ideas, culture, historical artefacts, art, fashion, food, language, and literature. Serious diseases spread around the globe. Scientists and horticulturalists shifted plants and animals from one part of the world to another.

It was the movement of goods such as tea, sugar and cotton, and wealth in the form of gold, silver and diamonds, that fuelled one of the greatest transformations in human history – the Industrial Revolution.

Keep or return?

Cultural art and artefacts were moved by the British Empire, mostly taken by force. They are still in Britain, where they are considered to be part of past history and it is suggested they are safest. The countries from which they came have asked for them to be returned. What do you think should happen to the items?

Benin Bronzes: These are 900 items demonstrating the long history and culture of Benin, taken from the palace in 1897, in an attack on the Oba (King) of the Kingdom of Benin in West Africa. They are currently on display at the British Museum.

Koh-i-Noor: This is the world's largest known diamond. In 1849, Duleep Singh, the ten-year-old heir to the throne of Punjab in India, was forced to sign a treaty which involved giving the Koh-i-Noor to the British. It became a special possession of Queen Victoria and was displayed at the 1851 Great Exhibition in London. It became part of the Crown Jewels and was last seen in 2002 on a crown that rested on the coffin of the Queen Mother.

Elgin Marbles: In the 1800s, Lord Elgin took the 2,500 marble statues and carvings from the Parthenon in Athens, Greece. These are currently in the care of the British Museum.

Can you make sense of these statements?

When the British *migrated to* parts of the Empire to rule over other people, and take control of their wealth, resources, and power it is seen by some people as **good thing**.

BUT

When people *migrated from* parts of the Empire into Britain, this was depicted by some as **negative**, even though the people who came were doing important, difficult jobs, and were contributing to Britain's wealth.

....

Britons living in the Empire – and around the world today – are called ex-pats.

BUT

British subjects from the Empire living in Britain are called immigrants.

....

British people living in, and ruling over, other countries **observed their British traditions** and kept themselves **separate** and **distinct** from the people who lived there. They rarely learnt local languages.

BUT

When migrants came to live here they were told **not to keep their own cultures** and they should be **more like the British** and try to fit in.

....

The reason the British ruled over colonies and dominions was so the people – as long as they were far away from Britain – could make money for Britain and make it rich.

BUT

If the same people are in Britain itself making money for Britain, then some people depict them as taking advantage of Britain and exploiting it.

....

In the British Empire, the movement of goods, people and money could happen easily and quickly, one of the reasons the British Empire became so powerful and wealthy. Today we call this "Freedom of Movement".

BUT

Freedom of movement is a hot topic today, with some people now saying it is a bad thing if people can come in and out of Britain easily.

Migration is the very thing that made Britain what it is today – by transporting people, power, resources, wealth, and ideas around the world. Every person we meet in Britain – me, your friends, your neighbours and, yes, even you – is a migrant in one form or another. And every story is as important, valuable, and human as the next.

Our collective history shows that migration connects all of us. Some of the stories are of adventure and wealth, others are some of the most painful and unjust you'll ever come across.

We can't jump in a time machine and go into the past to change all these migration stories, but we can have a conversation and get to know each other. We don't need a time machine for that.

Chapter Twelve

Terrific and terrifying technology

In the same way that the Empire created new companies and trade, it also led to the creation of new technology. This was good and bad for different people.

Queen Elizabeth I used the wealth looted by privateers to invest in naval technology (read more about privateers on page 204). From these beginnings, the English navy became superior, allowing it to fight and defeat enemies and to be faster and more direct for trade. The navy became England's competitive advantage to establishing its empire.

Steamships developed in the 19th century allowed travel inland up long rivers. That meant rapid expansion into Asia and Africa because there was no need to land at the coast and colonise the whole region.

In 1842, Britain used the world's biggest iron steamship, the *Nemesis*, as part of the Opium Wars, defeating the weaker Chinese ships.

Britain's powerful steam ships could travel into the vast Chinese interior to access raw materials, cheap labour and sell goods.

No wonder Britain's identity is so closely tied to its seafaring prowess. As the anthem goes, Britannia really did rule the waves (see page 176).

The Opium Wars

The East India Company wanted China's most prized commodity: tea. But China only exchanged tea for silver, which England didn't have. So instead, the East India Company smuggled opium into China and made the Company investors rich, and bought tea as well. But the addiction and death caused by the opium, led China to eventually crack down on the opium smuggling. In 1839 they confiscated and destroyed 20,000 chests of it. The British government sent warships to attack China. And because of Britain's naval superiority, the British easily won. China was forced to sign the Treaty of Nanjing in 1842. China had to pay Britain over £16 million and hand over the port of Hong Kong, which you'll remember was only returned to China in 1997. The First Opium War (1839–1842) was followed by the Second Opium War (1856–1860). The British won again, along with the French as part of their attack. The outcome was more concessions by China, such as legalising the opium trade, allowing free movement for Christian missionaries (see page 215), and opening all of China for trade with British companies.

BANG BANG BANG!

Sophisticated guns, weapons and bombs developed by the British were a big part of establishing British rule. For example, breechloading guns in the 1850s allowed British soldiers to load bullets quickly. Smokeless gunpowder in the 1880s meant soldiers didn't suffer the horrible consequences of smoke when firing.

And the British weren't shy about using their military tech, even when it wasn't necessary.

In 1879, after two years of fighting the Anglo-Zulu War in South Africa, ten British men were killed in the final battle compared to over 6,000 Zulus.

In 1898 the British massacred 11,000 Sudanese in Omdurman, while sustaining only 48 dead themselves.

In 1919, in a park called Jalian Wala Bagh, in Amritsar in India, the British army shot dead at least a thousand civilians, and hundreds more were injured, including children.

Naval and military technologies were used by the Empire to get resources, trade and to protect their people and goods. But they also used them to kill, injure and control many.

The technology was very effective. But it wasn't always a force for good.

Today, the UK is still one of the biggest exporters of arms in the world.

Spotlight on... the Falkland Islands

Off the coast of Argentina, the Falkland Islands have been a British Overseas Territory since 1833. It's been an ongoing dispute with Argentina, with a notable violent conflict in 1982. It is a strategic military location for Britain. And some see the islands as a remaining symbol of Britain's imperial power. The population is around 3,000, who voted in 2013 to remain part of Britain.

The story of quinine

When British people went out to grow the Empire, they would often be dead within a few months from malaria. However, some smart folks in Peru discovered that if the ground-up bark of their native cinchona tree was added to water and drunk regularly, it could prevent and cure malaria. But it tasted disgusting. In 1820 two French pharmacologists extracted quinine from the bark. When added to fizzy water it was easier to consume.

But Peru held a near monopoly on the cinchona trees. Some British adventurers **stole** cinchona saplings and smuggled them out of Peru. Britain created plantations in southern India, Malaya, and Indonesia to have its own quinine supply, which meant the Empire could grow more quickly. Some people say that without quinine there would be no British Empire.

Peru, France, Britain, India, Malaya, Indonesia, and commercial enterprise all played a role in developing and spreading a medicine to fight a deadly disease. It was a marvellous technological invention which has saved millions of lives. But it involved theft, slavery on plantations and made way for colonisation. Which means, like many technologies, how it was invented and its impact are complicated.

We have just lived through a global health pandemic. What lessons can we learn from the story of quinine to ensure that we work together to face health challenges, and that treatments benefit everyone, not just rich countries?

> **Gin and tonic**
>
> The alcoholic drink gin and tonic has come to symbolise Britishness because it would be drunk every afternoon in some parts of the world, to prevent malaria. The fizzy tonic water contained quinine. Winston Churchill said, "*Quinine saved more Englishmen's lives and minds, than all the doctors in the Empire.*"

The Industrial Revolution (1760–1840)

If you look around the room you're in now, many things you will see can trace their roots to the Industrial Revolution. Anything manufactured in a factory – that's your phone, computer, television, even the clothes you're wearing; anything mass produced that you probably buy in a shop.

The Industrial Revolution marked the transformation of goods from being created by hand to using machines. Some people say it's responsible for an increase in the population and a higher standard of living. Technology was at the heart of the Industrial Revolution.

1. invention of machines that could do work that had to be done by hand
2. the invention of new kinds of power – particularly steam power, but later also coal, oil, and gas
3. the invention of the factory system

You can see straight away that machines can manufacture products much faster than by hand. And in factories, more complex products could be made. And power also created speed, new ways of manufacturing things as well as transporting them.

The steam engine was first developed by Thomas Newcomen, and then improved by James Watt, a Scottish mechanic, in 1778. It meant that factories no longer needed to be built near rivers, as water had once been the source of power. Now they could be located anywhere, and the power was continuous and reliable. It could also be used for steam trains and steamships.

Cloth was England's key output. The invention of the spinning jenny meant production could massively increase. Credit for the spinning jenny, a hand-powered multiple spinning machine invented in 1764, goes to a British carpenter and weaver named James Hargreaves. His invention was the first machine to improve upon the spinning wheel. Instead of spinning thread one spindle at a time, as had always been done, the first spinning jennies had eight spindles, and later models had up to 120. The machines were too big to have in one home, and were moved to factories. Imagine how much thread could be spun now!

This was supported by machines like the water frame from Richard Arkwright, and the spinning mule from Samuel Crompton, speeding up cloth manufacture.

Arkwright is also said to have invented the modern-day factory in 1771. It was the first water-powered cotton-spinning mill and initially employed 200 workers. It ran day and night with two 12-hour shifts.

All of this changed the work people did – instead of owning their land for subsistence, they were now selling their "labour" and their conditions were dependent on the business owners. They also only usually worked on one part of the process of manufacture. The government felt business owners should be able to treat their workers as they wanted, as they apparently knew best how to make profit, and that the government should leave them to it (called *laissez faire*). But all of this led to discontent among working people and the rise of the labour movement, trade unions and protests (see page 114).

It also highlighted differences in new "classes" of people. Businessmen, who established factories and trade who became wealthy and known as the industrial capitalists, and the middle classes. Those who worked were called – you guessed it – the working classes.

But let's come back to our discussion of the inventions of the Industrial Revolution. Their impact can't be understated, and something transformative happened in Britain that impacted all human experience going forward. Which means that there's no doubt that there were brilliant British inventors and businesspeople. But the Industrial Revolution could only have happened because of the resources of the Empire and cheap and free labour from around the world and the working classes. Being proud of those inventions is important, but so is recognising what really went into making the technological revolution a success.

Cotton cloth

In the 1750s a new industry emerged in Britain: cotton cloth.

The raw cotton was picked by enslaved people in the Caribbean plantations. It was brought to Britain where the new machines processed it. The work in the factories was done by the working class. In the UK, people found themselves forced to leave the countryside due to enclosure laws (see page 127). They looked for work in the new manufacturing cities. In the factories they worked long hours in dangerous conditions, and lived in terrible homes. Even children as young as four worked. They did not have any rights, and employers did not have to take care of their safety. Employers said this was okay because otherwise they wouldn't make a profit.

The cloth was sold around the world. The business owners, traders and the government got rich! Some cloth was even sold in Africa, from where enslaved people had been kidnapped – and the money used to buy more enslaved people. The cotton manufacturing industry in India was deliberately weakened by the British so that there would be no competition.

The Industrial Revolution meant the growth of factories, burning of fossil fuels, pollution, and damage to the environment by changing the crops grown. All of this has affected the world and climate change.

Nobody thought about those possible impacts and their enormous negative effects. But we can learn lessons whenever we develop new technologies today, and ask ourselves what impacts they might have on the world.

Spotlight on... the Caribbean

The Caribbean was already home to indigenous people like the Taino, Carib, and Arawak, but they were killed by European explorers who used violence or brought diseases like smallpox. The British developed plantations to cultivate vast quantities of crops, tended to by enslaved people. Some of the largest plantations of the whole of the British Empire were in the Caribbean, growing sugar, tobacco and cotton. Jamaica was one of the largest and most profitable.

"Next stop: Big bucks for Britain": the story of the Indian railways

Steam trains were invented in 1825. This allowed the British Empire to move goods to its ports, so they could ship them more easily around the world.

Railways were soon laid across India, based on a plan by the East India Company to transport iron ore, tea, cotton, coal and other goods from India's interior to its seaports. The railways were also used to transport soldiers to the different Indian regions to maintain control.

The UK's private investors were happy to put money into the railways because the government ensured there was no risk, and it was the Indians who were paying for the railways to be built.

But today the story of the railways, which brought immense profit and wealth to Britain, is retold as though the railways were in fact given as a gift to India. It wasn't a gift to the Indians, even though it might be an important part of the country now. We should just be honest about that. After all, when the railways were built, it was for the benefit of the Empire.

"Hello, is that the Empire speaking?"

The invention of communications technology 200 years ago led to a unified, global British Empire. Now all the parts of the Empire could be in quick communication, adding speed and superiority to its military services.

After radio was invented, the BBC was used to solidify a British identity around the world. In the corners of the Empire, people could hear the sound of "home" and feel a sense of belonging through the BBC World Service. It started broadcasting in other languages too, so the British perspective came to dominate global news. Compared to the armed services, this is called "soft power" and this influence can still be seen today.

A force for global good?

The British Empire is a great example of the power that technology can give you, as well as the responsibilities that come with developing it.

We didn't do it all on our own. We used the wealth, talents and resources of all the people and lands of the Empire. Although it's fair to say that technologies like communications and health did ultimately benefit humankind as a whole, many were also harmed. This has left a mark on those people. We need to recognise and learn from these.

Britain clearly has a talent for technology. We should draw on our heritage for innovation and ensure Britain continues to be a great place to nurture magnificent new technologies for the future.

There's a whole new wave of important technologies coming up. Agricultural technology could ensure we have enough food for the world's population. Space technologies will open new horizons for us. Medicines and health technology can help us fight pandemics. Green technologies can save the planet.

This time, instead of richer countries taking advantage of these technologies for themselves, we need collaborative creative solutions.

If you become a scientist, inventor, or entrepreneur you can do things differently this time, and ensure technology is a force for *everyone's good*.

P.S. If you do, in fact, have a technology to solve climate change, please let everyone share it, okay?

Part Three

The story of now

Watch out for these words

Apartheid – the law that applied in South Africa from 1948–1994 that enforced legal superiority of white-skinned people, and kept everyone else separate and legally inferior (see page 214).

Civilising mission – the goal of trying to "improve" people, because you think you are superior, and they are inferior.

Deport – to expel someone from a country, typically on the grounds that they are there illegally, or have committed a crime.

"Divide and rule" – the name of the strategy used by the British Empire to keep control of colonies, in particular India. The aim is to divide existing groups, so they fight each other, and therefore allow the British to take control, sometimes with the excuse that the British are needed to keep the peace.

Dominion – a country that is part, or was once part, of the British Empire.

Merchant Navy – the ships used for trade and transporting goods.

Postcolonialism – describes the thoughts, politics and literature of a place that used to be a colony.

Chapter Thirteen

Hitting the fast forward button

As Britain emerged from the World Wars, it was almost bankrupt, and running an empire was an expensive and time-consuming business. It just didn't have the money or resources to do so. Countries under its rule had been fighting for independence for a long time and they were becoming harder to control. Many had been promised independence in return for contributing troops and resources to Britain's efforts in the World Wars (see *photo section*). The poor treatment of the soldiers from those countries made them even more determined to secure it when they returned home.

The public mood in Britain was also shifting away from empires and ruling over other states by force, towards ideas of people having liberation and self-determination. Global attitudes were changing too. Britain's allies in World War II, such as the USA, supported decolonisation. This put pressure on countries like Britain and France to end their imperial activities. One by one, the colonies fought for and won their independence.

Spotlight on... the United Kingdom and Ireland
England annexed Wales towards the end of the 13th century after a lot of conflict. Next was Scotland, with the Act of Union in 1707 which made Scotland, England, and Wales into one nation: Great Britain. The Acts of Union of 1801 united Britain with Ireland to form the United Kingdom of Great Britain and Ireland. But there was ongoing Irish resistance and rebellions, and in 1922, Ireland got its independence, but Northern Ireland remained as part of the United Kingdom.

Britain continued to have relationships with its ex-colonies. In fact, many people were invited to live in Britain to help rebuild the post-war nation, because the country was desperate for workers. These included people sometimes described today as the Windrush Generation (see page 211). Some came from parts of the Empire and Commonwealth as economic migrants under their rights as British overseas citizens and under the laws which welcomed them. This included my family who felt they were simply moving from one part of Britain to another. Britain also welcomed refugees from its ex-colonies, like the Ugandan Asians who were persecuted by the country's new leader.

In 1926, the idea of the Commonwealth was established between Britain and some of its dominions. They agreed that all nations were *equal in status, in no way subordinate one to another in any aspect of their domestic or external affairs, though united by common allegiance to the Crown.* Although it's worth remembering that this was also the time that Britain was at its peak of size and power as an empire ruling over others. The Commonwealth was headed up by the British king, George VI. He was the grandfather of the current king, Charles III. The organisation grew as newly independent British ex-colonies joined, and today there is a current membership of 54. Almost all of these were once part of the British Empire.

"We are here, because you were there"

Unfortunately, when those who had been part of the British Empire, and contributed to Britain's wealth, and who were even invited to come here, actually arrived, the experience was often very hostile. I know from my own parents that they faced racism for being South Asian (as have I) and what happened to them isn't unusual.

There were attacks on black- and brown-skinned people, including by police. There were extremely offensive signs that said things like "No coloureds" or "No Irish, no blacks, no dogs". There were even cases of famous politicians and election campaigns being run by saying openly racist things. It seemed to be OK for these people to work towards making Britain wealthy, and provide goods and troops, as long as it was "over there" in the colonies that once made up the British Empire. There's a famous saying in Britain that "*We are only here, because you were over there.*" Some people still feel hostile to migrants today.

In fact, many people then – and still today – are told to "go back home". But for many families, home is Britain and, because of the British Empire, it has been for hundreds of years. That's why in the previous chapter I put my heart on to the page and explained how important it is to create a sense of Britishness, no matter people's origins, that makes this feel like home, and that people truly belong.

It's hard for me to talk about this, but I am often told to my face that this isn't my home, and that I don't belong here. It's one of the most painful things you can be told, when you've poured your life and love into a place. As my lovely readers, I want you to promise me that you will never, *ever* say anything like that. In fact, I'd like you to work hard to make sure people really do feel like this is home.

There are also many uplifting stories from people who have found their homes in Britain, had families, an education, and opportunities. Today many have become politicians, actors, celebrities, scientists, sportspeople, businesspeople and are part of every aspect of British life.

A new shape to the world

Have you ever looked at a map of Africa and wondered why there are so many countries with straight borders? I have. The way human beings adapt to landscapes is usually shaped by wiggly rivers or jagged mountain ranges, not to mention groups of people whose villages don't usually happen along straight lines.

This puzzled me for a long time, until I discovered that a lot of countries didn't exist in the form they are today, until colonial powers – like the British Empire – literally got a map and drew lines on it. In some cases, some European powers decided to carve up land between them, as though the land belonged to them, not the people who actually lived there! They weren't concerned about whether there were natural borders, or where people's towns and villages were.

At the Berlin Conference in 1884, the USA and 14 European countries, including Britain, came together to discuss how to divide up Africa's resources between them. There weren't any representatives from Africa! How would you feel if you were from Africa and other people were deciding how to divide up the place *you* live and share out *your* resources and wealth?

On top of dividing up the lands, and helping themselves to its wealth, the countries at the Berlin Conference agreed that they needed to bring "civilisation" to Africa in the form of Christianity (see page 215 for more about the civilising mission.) Similar discussions about carving up other parts of the world happened for the Middle East, and East and Southeast Asia.

In the area of East Africa that my family are from, my mum would recount how her dad had German banknotes, but then they became useless. I couldn't make any sense of this for a long time – where did German money come from in Tanganyika (today's Tanzania), which was run by the British? That is, until

I learnt very recently that the Germans and British fought over and then agreed how to divide up East Africa. After World War I, at the Treaty of Versailles, Germany was forced to hand over its overseas colonies. But not to the people who lived there – to other European nations. The family story of the banknotes is one experience of how ordinary people were affected by other countries deciding who would control them.

This explains a lot about why there is often conflict between countries today. It's not that people who were once colonised by the Empire like fighting and that the Empire brought them peace and stability. One of the reasons is because of the way the borders didn't take account of how people live and how resources are shared. In some cases, large groups of people were simply divided, leading to situations today where they want to unite again and create their own state.

Goodbye from Britain

Many of the conflicts, civil wars, and instability we see around the world can trace their origins to the way countries were set up when Britain departed. Sometimes it's due to the way borders were created. In others, new countries were left without resources, because they had been drained by the Empire as it left. Or they had been turned into commodity-dependent nations. What this means is that Britain had deliberately transformed the landscape to focus on producing a few or just one kind of crop, instead of the normal way a country would operate, by having lots of different kinds of sources of income, as well as being able to provide food for its own people. This means that if the price of those specific crops goes down, or even fails, the country no longer has ways to generate money.

The legacy of the time the British had spent in an area is still likely to be woven into the legal systems and laws the British introduced, which still affect those countries today. It would have impacted the languages people speak, as well as the local rivalries inflamed by "divide and rule" strategies.

To run a country, you need things called a "machinery of state" which include the organisations, rules and processes that a government needs to make laws and run the country smoothly. As Britain left, there was often no proper machinery of state established, so it's no surprise there was chaos after the British left.

"Poof!" goes the paperwork

It's been discovered recently that historical papers in the countries once part of the Empire were destroyed on purpose by the British as they left. Those papers would have given us information about what the British had done in those countries. But those memories were not preserved, and perhaps they wanted those memories to be forgotten. In the last few years, the important documents of the Windrush Generation, and their connection to the Empire, were also destroyed.

Lines that divide: the tragedy of Partition

When the British left India, they created one of the biggest and most horrendous cases of division: **Partition**. India was divided into two countries – India and Pakistan. The latter aimed to be a homeland for Muslims, who were in the minority in India. Pakistan itself was in two parts: West and East Pakistan, and they weren't even connected! The British were meant to withdraw in a slow and orderly way, but they announced that they were leaving in a matter of weeks in 1947. They announced India's independence three days before they announced the border between India and Pakistan! So, nobody even knew where exactly each country began or ended! As a result, people had to flee overnight to get to the country they wanted to be in. The man who drew the border between India and Pakistan, Cyril Radcliffe, had never been to the area. So, it was no surprise with such little time, and knowledge that Partition didn't take account of ethnicities, communities and cities.

Up to 14 million people moved, one of the largest migrations in human history. Sadly, because of the "divide and rule" strategy the British had implemented, violence broke out between different religious groups and more than a million people were killed.

The same issues caused further division between West and East Pakistan. A civil war between them eventually led to East Pakistan declaring itself as the independent nation of Bangladesh.

It's also worth noting that what was once the prosperous and wealthy province of Bengal (that spans today's India and Bangladesh) had already been split by the British in 1905 into West and East Bengal, as another part of the "divide and rule" strategy.

Today, there are still serious tensions between India and Pakistan, and a war over the disputed territory of Kashmir still rages.

New nation states emerged in the Middle East that had never existed before, and we still see violence and struggle over them today. In 1926, the Balfour Declaration laid the foundations for the future state of Israel as a "national home for Jewish people" in an area that had long been recognised as Palestine, including by the British. Many Arab leaders were angry because they had been expecting independence after supporting the British to fight the Ottomans.

All of which give a taste of the fact that the stories that Britain tells about how it gave independence to its colonies is not necessarily the experience they had when they fought for and won it.

Spotlight on... India

Today's country of India is in fact one part of the area that was British India at the time. When the English arrived in 1608 in Surat, Gujarat, the Mughal Empire ruled over large parts of India, and it was at the peak of its power. There was also a series of regional kingdoms. The Mughals were one of the richest empires of the time alongside the Ottomans in Turkey, the Safavids in Persia, and the Ming dynasty in China. It was known for its cultural and artistic achievements and administration and governance. And how rich it was!

Eventually, as British control over India grew, the area included today's India, Pakistan, Bangladesh, and Sri Lanka, as well as parts of Myanmar and Nepal. Sir Robert Clive is credited for establishing the Raj in India, the Empire's "jewel in the crown". But he was also responsible for the exploitation, oppression and deaths of millions of Indians.

Britain and Russia had long fought over Afghanistan, in a conflict called the Great Game. The British Empire and the Russian Empire had an ongoing power struggle with wars and treaties over central Asia, as both wanted access to resources in the region. Britain wanted to protect its power over India. You can see echoes of the Great Game today in who controls or influences the region.

Spotlight on... the Middle East

In the early 17th century, England built trade relations with the Ottoman Empire, which controlled most of the Middle East. In 1839, the East India Company occupied Aden, a port in today's Yemen. It became a key regional centre for British operations. Keeping British routes to India secure was important. The Anglo-Persian war (1856–1857) aimed to stop Persia's power. In 1882, Britain occupied Egypt after the first Suez Canal Crisis. Britain and France secretly signed the Sykes-Picot Agreement (1916) dividing up the Ottoman Empire's Arab territories. In the 19th and 20th centuries, the Gulf region made treaties with Britain: in return for the "Qawasim pirates" giving safe passage to British ships, it would give financial and military support to the Trucial states. Britain created the Anglo-Persian Oil Company in 1901 (later called BP). It made a lot of money. Persia (today's Iran) wanted to profit from its own oil, so wanted to nationalise the industry. With Britain's support, a coup was planned against the democratically elected leader, and the previous Shah – more favourable to the British – was reinstated.

Goodbye from the other side

If your family and your country have been ruled over by another for a long time, your resources are taken, and you're told that you are inferior, it can leave very long-lasting trauma for you. It also leaves huge damage – socially, economically, and politically – on your country. You may have lost people in fights for independence, and suffered war and imprisonment. It totally changes the way you think about yourself.

The historical period of the aftermath of the Empire is sometimes called **postcolonialism** – that is "post" (after) and "colonialism" (when a country takes control of another land). This word can also refer to the study of the lasting impacts of empire. Countries and people are spending a lot of time researching and thinking about these impacts, especially in trying to create stability and prosperity for themselves.

When countries first started to win independence, the process was called **decolonisation**. Today that word is often used to talk about reclaiming identity and sense of self, particularly to reject the sense of inferiority that was instilled by the British Empire into groups of people and countries to justify its control.

That means asking hard questions about whether Britain really was superior. For example, were the countries it colonised inferior? India had the biggest economy in the world when Britain arrived, but was in debt when it left. Africa wasn't full of savages; it was home to civilisations with their own legal systems, libraries, language, art, and culture. We know this because British colonisers stole this wealth, art and culture and brought it to England (see page 133 about the Benin Bronzes, Elgin Marbles and Koh-i-Noor).

You might even hear about **"decolonising the curriculum"** in Britain. This is a discussion about whether new, missing stories should be included in lessons taught in schools and universities, that give different perspectives rather than the traditional ones told from the viewpoint of the British Empire.

And what about Britain?

In the same way that the world and the colonies have moved on with their journeys, has Britain moved on? Well, of course it has. The country has changed dramatically and so have its people. So then the real question is, has Britain changed its idea of itself to reflect these changes, and does it share a new perspective on what happened during the Empire and how others see its imperial legacy?

Sometimes people say that Britain has "historical amnesia" about its past, which is a fancy way of saying it forgot the terrible things it did, but does remember what it thinks are the good parts.

There seems to be a gap between Britain's idea of itself, and how the world sees Britain today. One of the reasons this gap exists is because there are lots of stories we've never heard, which could help our understanding of what the Empire was.

And that's exactly what we are about to explore – the stories that are hidden in plain sight all around us, the stories that remain untold (including yours!) and why it is important to hear them.

Chapter Fourteen

Once upon a time there was an empire...

If you're a football fan, you might know that the original Wembley Stadium opened in 1923 and hosted its first ever FA Cup final just four days later. But did you know it was actually built to host the British Empire Exhibition from 1924–1925, to create a sense of pride in the vast might of the British Empire?

Built in classical style, it featured Mughal Indian architecture, to show Britain's imperial power.

It was demolished in 2003, replaced with today's huge white metal arch. The road is still called Empire Way. The base of the stadium flagpole is in a local park.

Why am I telling you this story? I want you to see for yourself that the British Empire is **hidden in plain sight all around us**.

Your city might be founded or shaped in some way by the Empire, the buildings built from the Empire's wealth, or to administer it. Your food may draw its origins from the Empire, or created from the goods of the Empire's plantations, and colonial trade.

The buildings around us

Many of the country homes and estates across Britain were built, furnished, decorated, and maintained by the wealth of the Empire. The National Trust is Europe's biggest conservation charity, and looks after hundreds of historic properties in the UK. It has released a report showing that over 90 of its properties have links to slavery and British colonialism, inviting people to explore this part of their heritage.

There may be buildings near you that were built to serve the Empire, or were paid for by its wealth. Why not find out more?

Some of the country's biggest banks and businesses made money due to slavery, and this money was put into cultural projects. These include the Tate Gallery, the Victoria & Albert Museum, and the British Museum. Their grand buildings are a record of the wealth the Empire generated, as well as showcasing the millions of cultural artefacts taken from the colonies. Many of those countries would like their objects back!

How many things in your daily life can you spot that have their origins in the British Empire? It's probably a lot more than you think!

Words of Empire

Do you enjoy summer BARBECUES or a paddle in a CANOE? These words are taken from the Caribbean. NUGGET is from Australia. GINGHAM is from Malaya and was once called *genggang* or *gengyang*.

If you're wearing PYJAMAS while doing YOGA on the VERANDAH of your BUNGALOW, then thank India.

When it comes to horror movies, are you screaming or hiding? Either way, watch out for ZOMBIES and VOODOO, originally from West Africa.

The reason that Britain used to have a coin called the GUINEA, made of gold, is because the gold came from a West African country called... you guessed it, Guinea.

Cities of Empire

During the 19th century London grew from 1 million people to over six million, the world's largest city, due to the Empire's trade.

Liverpool and Bristol grew rich as slave ports, and hubs for people travelling across the Empire. Glasgow's wealth came from managing the contracts of slavery and Empire goods, without the trading or port.

Factories became a feature due to the Industrial Revolution. Manchester was called "Cottonopolis" because cotton from the Empire was turned into textiles here and clothing was shipped back to the colonies to make more money. The Black Country in the West Midlands was so called because of its coal mining industry, and the factories that produced soot, all of which was part of the Industrial Revolution.

Celebrating through anthems and titles

You might have hummed along with rousing hymns and anthems, often sung at big national events. "Rule, Britannia!" speaks of Britain's story as a sea power. "Land of Hope and Glory" is about celebrating the vastness and ongoing growth of the Empire.

Some say they are no longer relevant to us today, and in fact are upsetting. "Rule, Britannia" has a line that says, "Britons never, never, never shall be slaves" but this was written when Britain was enslaving other people. The song "Land of Hope and Glory" talks about the Empire being "wider still, and wider", which reflects a Britain that wished to colonise more and more lands. Is that still relevant to the country we are today?

Do you fancy being given a title by the King from the Most Excellent Order of the British Empire to recognise your contribution to Britain? It's nice to be recognised by your country, isn't it? But some people have rejected these awards, saying that being associated with the Empire isn't a matter of honour because so many people were enslaved (sometimes their own ancestors) and we don't even have an Empire anymore. One suggestion is to change it to the Order of British "Excellence". But others say we should keep this important historic tradition.

History re-remembered

In the summer of 2020, along with millions of people around the world, I watched reports of Edward Colston's statue being removed from Bristol's centre and toppled into the sea (see *photo section*). It was an event filled with many different emotions: anger, relief, shame, freedom, satisfaction, rage...

I know that I'm the author of a book about the British Empire, but until that day I'd never heard of Edward Colston. I suspect lots of other people hadn't either. So why did his statue matter so much?

The things we choose to occupy our public spaces show us WHO WE ARE AS A NATION and what kind of people and qualities are important to us. Statues celebrate the people we see as heroes. But how and why are they chosen?

Colston lived from 1636 to 1721, becoming wealthy as a slave trader. He put some of his money back into the development of the city of Bristol, the slave port that made him rich. Over a hundred years after his death, in 1895, it was decided to erect a statue of him in Bristol. To the people of that time, Colston portrayed a positive, dominant British Empire, part of the Victorian push to justify the Empire. They made no mention of his links to slavery.

In 2020, his story – like that of the British Empire more generally – was being interpreted again. Today, many see Colston as a man who made money from the enslavement of 100,000 people and the deaths of 20,000 more, as they were transported from Africa to the West Indies. So was the statue a celebration of being a rich, empire-builder who gave money to improve the lives of people in his home city? Or is the statue a remembrance of cruelty, slavery, and stolen wealth? Today, there are many, many statues all over the country that ask similar questions of us. Is there one near where you live? If so, who is that person? What was their story? How do you feel about them representing your local town?

What should happen to our statues?

Which of these statements to do you think is the right approach?

Leave them as they are. History should remain as it is so we can remember our past.

We should leave them alone but add more information about them for people to read.

They should be replaced with statues of people who are more relevant to the nation we are today.

They should be moved to a museum where they can be explained and viewed as objects of history and art.

Who decides what's in our public spaces?

Earlier, I told you the story of how the original Wembley Stadium was demolished in 2003. But what do you think happened to it?

The rubble was moved and turned into four large earth mounds in a London suburb called Northala Fields. I've stood on those anonymous hills. Compared to the heated emotions about Edward Colston's statue, it made me wonder why are some memories more important than others? And who gets to decide?

Our public space should reflect all of us and who we are today, which means the answer is that it must be a collective discussion that considers all parts of our history: the victors, the villains, the colonisers and the colonised, and the secrets hidden in the rubble.

Chapter Fifteen

Missing stories

Imagine a family picture you particularly love that has you in it, or a class photo with you and all your friends, or a video of a special party you attended with you at the centre of the film.

Now look again. This time the family picture has a blank space instead of you. The class photo has been cropped, so only the other students appear. You've been completely airbrushed from the film.

Fast forward 10, 50, 100 or maybe 500 years. Someone is collecting histories about your family, your school or that big occasion. But you are not in those photos. You are missing from that story. Nobody knows anything about you or the impact you had on the family, class or event. A historian couldn't really have a true idea of what happened if you were removed from the stories.

How would you feel if future-you discovered you were missing? You and your descendants would rightly be upset that your history and contribution was missing, and angry at the people who erased you and your story, or made up different stories about you. You'd think about why and how they had the power to do that.

In the telling of the tales of the British Empire, there are blanks where there should be stories – stories that were never collected or which have been altered.

If we want to understand the *Story of Now*, we need to understand **all the parts** of what happened in the past. So how do we do that? By collecting stories and sharing them.

Stories of the enslaved

Around 1759, a little boy called Olaudah, aged 10 – perhaps a similar age to you – was kidnapped from his village in southern Nigeria and sold into the transatlantic slave trade. Eventually he made it to London as a free man and learnt to read and write. His memoir, *The Interesting Narrative of the Life of Olaudah Equiano,* published in 1789, became a bestseller, one of the first stories about the actual experience of being a slave (see *photo section*). It was when people could read real accounts of slavery, that they truly understood how terrible it was to enslave people. He became a leading abolitionist, and his story was one of the triggers in the eventual laws that ended slavery (see page 67 for more about abolition).

The fact he was skilled in writing helped change the course of history and millions of lives. Writing stories can be a superhero skill!

The language we use to tell stories

Not only do we need more stories, we also need to think about the language we use to describe what happened. For example, in 1857 in India, there was a huge uprising against the British called the "Indian Mutiny". This is a description by the British of what those in power think happened. And if something is a mutiny then it suggests there is a right to crush it. But later people started calling it the "First War of Independence" which makes it feel very different – the struggle of the people of India to reclaim their country.

All the descriptions we use are always up for discussion – even the ways that I've described things in this book! Because our ideas and perspectives are always developing, and new stories are a powerful way to do that.

Hearing all sides of the story

Most of the histories we have of the British Empire are written from a British perspective. But what about the stories of the colonised – the people who were ruled over?

At an exhibition at the Birmingham Museum and Art Gallery in 2017 there was a small glass cabinet with a handmade blood-stained knife and a homemade rifle. A letter from a curator in 1964 says, "*I thought they might make an amusing addition of a specialist sort to our African collections.*" He found it funny that people were defending themselves with such basic weapons. But is it still funny when you learn the rest of the story? The weapons were used in the Mau Mau Kikuyu Rebellion in Kenya between 1952–1960.

Since the 1920s British settlers had taken over most of the Kikuyu land, and in the end the Kikuyu people decided to fight back. The British declared this a rebellion and about 12,000 Kenyans were killed. 1,000 "rebels" were hanged and more than 100,000 were sent to prison camps. The prisoners were not allowed to write letters about their treatment. Paperwork by the government that authorised the policies was destroyed. So, we never knew their side of the story.

In recent years their stories of brutal beatings and torture were eventually told, changing the perception of the whole event from a rebellion to a brutal massacre. The new stories led to compensation by the UK government to the many innocent Kikuyu who were killed or tortured.

Doesn't a new perspective make a difference?

Spotlight on... Australia

In 1788, the British founded Sydney, almost two decades after Captain James Cook claimed southeast Australia for Britain. Migration to Australia increased for different reasons: transportation of criminals, the discovery of gold, the chance for economic and agricultural opportunity. Britain took advantage of Australia's raw materials like gold, wool, iron, and coal to use in manufacturing, along with the food it grew. Australia was also a big market for Britain's manufactured goods. And Australia provided troops to Britain, especially in the World Wars. Of course, this all came at a price to the Aboriginal Australians who continue to suffer the consequences today. Disease and violence eradicated many. Their lands were forcibly taken. In fact, the British said Australia was "Terra Nullius" meaning "empty land", claiming no one lived there! Perhaps the most heart-breaking was the British policy of removing Aboriginal children from their families by force so they would not remember their own culture. These children are called the "stolen generations".

Stories of resistance

There were different kinds of resistance and rebellions right across the different areas and periods of the British Empire. In 1776, the thirteen colonies of the country we know today as the United States of America declared independence. But it came as part of a series of wars as the American colonists tried to break free from Britain.

On the other side of the world, in Tasmania, the British fought the "Black Wars" against the indigenous Tasmanian Aboriginal people. They took over the hunting areas, and kidnapped and murdered the locals. The wars lasted from 1804 into the 1930s, and by the end, there were almost no Aboriginal people left.

In today's Zimbabwe, Mbuya Nehanda led the First Chimurenga (uprising) in 1896–1897, part of local resistance against the British. They assassinated her, but on her death she said defiantly, "*My bones will rise again*." The British took Nehanda's bones back to Britain as a trophy of their triumph and her humiliation. But her words became a rallying cry for the Second Chimurenga (uprising) in 1966–1979, which led to the independence of Zimbabwe. She is considered a national hero, and in 2022 the government of Zimbabwe sent an official delegation to Britain to ask for the return of her remains.

The relationship of Ireland and England, and then Britain, went back all the way to the 13th century when the English arrived there. Some even point to that as the first seeds of the future British Empire. In fact, it's hard to capture in a few sentences the longstanding relationship and resistance. There were Irish uprisings from the 16th century onwards, a rebellion in 1798 inspired by the American Revolution. The Act of Union legally joined Britain and Ireland together in 1801. In 1845–1852, Ireland was devastated by the Irish Potato Famine. 1 million people died, and a further 1 million emigrated. Resistance to British rule was constant and continued. In 1922, the Irish Civil War led to the division of Ireland, as southern Ireland asserted its independence from Britain, while Northern Ireland stayed as part of the United Kingdom.

Within Britain

When stories of the Empire are told, it is about the grand achievements. Even this book started by telling you how huge the Empire was. But Britain wasn't just about the colonisers, kings, and queens. Most people were from what we might call the working classes. In 1841 around three quarters of the UK population worked in factories, on the land or as domestic servants. But we just don't know much at all about these people because most of these stories were never recorded.

I tried to look up "working class history of the British Empire" and guess what? It doesn't seem to exist. But in Britain, it was the working class that provided the labour for factories and mills, for the navy and military. Maybe you could write that history?

Regional voices

There's also a huge gap from the different regions of Britain: Scotland, Wales, and Northern Ireland, as well as the regions of England. The British Empire had so many different impacts. Some regions lost their rural agriculture, and manufacturing cities grew from the Industrial Revolution. Railways and canals were built. The ports and coastal cities sprung up. Then the Empire declined – and with it manufacturing, mining, commerce, transport and more, but the buildings and the canals remain. Are there any of these reminders of Empire where you live? What story do they tell about the history of your hometown?

Opposition

As you've been reading this book you might think everybody in Britain was waving their cheerleading pompoms for the British Empire. But, there was all sorts of opposition, anger, horror and shame. The stories of these people are not as well known.

Today, it can feel like the only options are to be either fully for, or fully opposed to the Empire, without room to discuss those people who have other perspectives. But the history of the British Empire was filled with people disagreeing or asking difficult questions. Maybe the most British thing you can do is to ask tough questions, and you don't always have to agree.

Women

Imagine the history of the British Empire was missing the stories of Queen Victoria or Elizabeth I. Unthinkable, right! But this is exactly what has happened to the stories of hundreds of millions of women. Empire wasn't just male explorers, privateers, rulers, and merchants! Women shaped the Empire and were shaped by it.

Pioneering women went out to the colonies and laboured the land. Some women were involved in the matters of government and state. Gertrude Bell, for example, played an influential role mediating for the British government in the Middle East. Some women went as wealthy wives, creating a piece of Britain far away from home, and establishing the hierarchy between the British and the colonised. They had female servants and instead of seeing sisterhood, they often oppressed them. And let's not forget hundreds of millions of women were colonised, enslaved or indentured by the British Empire.

Women often went out to parts of the Empire in search of a husband with a good colonial job and steady income. They were called the "Fishing Fleet".

In some periods of the British Empire, British men were forbidden from marrying local women and had to marry British women to preserve British identity and racial separation.

Children

In the early 19th century, there were more than a million child workers including 350,000 seven- to ten-year-olds in England alone. They made up 15% of the total workforce. Many weren't paid, just given very basic food and a bed.

The Industrial Revolution needed labour, and small bodies to do fiddly work or get into cramped places. Child labour was their answer – cheap, small and easy to exploit.

A large part of the wealth that the mines and factories generated during the Industrial Revolution was created by children *just like you*. But it took a heavy toll on their health, education, and life expectancy.

It was only when oral stories were collected – including from the children themselves, some as young as five – that laws were passed to protect children.

"As a child I worked from five in the morning till nine at night. It was so dusty, the dust got up my lungs, and the work was so hard. I got so bad in health, that when I pulled the baskets down, I pulled my bones out of their places."

Elizabeth Bentley, 1832
on working in a flax mill starting at the age of 6

"It is very laborious employment; pieceners are continually running to and fro, and on their feet the whole day. It is commonly very difficult to keep up with the work. It makes them bleed, the skin is completely rubbed off, and in that case they bleed perhaps in a dozen parts. I generally was beaten when I happened to be too late."

Matthew Crabtree, 1832,
on working as a piecener from 8 years old

When children told their own stories and were listened to, it changed their lives, and the lives of other children of the time. The novels of Charles Dickens include many children living and working in poverty, and those taking advantage of them to make money. You might be familiar with *Oliver Twist*, *Bleak House* or *A Christmas Carol*, which was inspired by these stories. In fact, Dickens himself became a child labourer at the age of 12 when his father fell into debt and was sent to prison. He had to work at a shoe-blacking factory for 10–12 hours every day. Elizabeth Gaskell wrote *North and South*, which featured children working in the dangerous cotton mills of a fictional town based on Manchester. These are stories that still shape our thinking about children and poverty today.

So, when you're outside in the playground, or resting at the weekend, take a minute to think about how those children, bravely and honestly telling their stories, changed the course of history, and your life too.

Erasure, error and endeavour

While I was writing this book I kept thinking to myself, "*I mustn't forget this country... What about that territory... I need to mention these people and what they did...*" because one of the biggest challenges of telling a history as vast in time and place as that of the

British Empire is avoiding **erasure**. This is when voices, stories, places, people and events are literally erased from history because we don't try to find them, or perhaps even exclude them, and, because of this, they don't feature in our conversations now. One of the things often raised in discussions about the British Empire is this erasure of people and places.

So, you can imagine how nervous I felt when writing this book, about forgetting something, and trying to include as many stories as I can. But it's probable that I've not mentioned people and places that deserved to have been included. After all, this is just one short book!

And as our ideas and information about what happened grow, it's possible that what I've written will need to be updated or even corrected. I've tried my best. And knowing that I've tried my best, I hope you'll give me the benefit of the doubt, and help me fill in the blanks. As time passes, we might start to use words, languages and ideas differently from the way I've used them in my writing. Again, I've tried my best with what I'm aware of at this time. Maybe we'll all find better ways together to talk about our stories in the most sensitive and compassionate ways possible.

Because the whole idea of the book is to give *you* the starting point to explore more. And if your story, or a place you're interested in or connected to isn't here, I hope you'll write those stories and be part of this journey we are on together.

YOU HAVE THE POWER!

The stories told *by* children like you make a difference. But the stories told *to* children also make a difference. Because they go on to shape our thinking about the world. So don't be afraid of questioning the stories you are told. And be brave about looking for new perspectives. Just like the ones we have heard from the children in this book. But what I want you to take from this chapter is that if you want to properly understand Britain, the British Empire, and your life, it's important to look for new stories, especially the ones we haven't heard. Including yours.

Chapter Sixteen

A heated debate

It's the 21st century and the world has changed. Britain is no longer an empire. And the world itself has reached a postcolonial era. Having an empire is extremely out of fashion. Power and wealth have shifted. Many of the countries once ruled over by Britain and other colonial powers are now growing in economy, culture, political and social influence. Britain, the many and diverse people who live there and modern British culture, are also very different.

All of this means we can't really expect Britain to be the same country today that it was a hundred years ago. And we can't expect the people in it to think, feel or act in the same way. People are talking about who we are *today*, what we'd like other people to think about us, and the role we want to play in the world.

Sounds simple enough, right?

WRONG!

It's not simple at all. Instead, it can be a very heated debate.

Here are some of the kinds of things people say:

> The British Empire did a lot of good in the world by sharing Britain's language, literature, education, government systems, legal system and railways.

> The British Empire made people's lives worse through slavery, taking their resources and their cultures, and removing their own power to decide for themselves how to live.

> The British Empire improved the lives of the people who were part of it and so those people should be happy.

We wouldn't like being part of another empire. We're proud of Boudicca for trying to reclaim independence from the Romans, even though they gave us roads and aqueducts.

The British Empire was an incredible achievement, superior and more significant than any empire previously. We should have the same pride in the British Empire that we had a hundred years ago.

The British Empire did horrible things to be big, powerful and rich. We need to be honest and admit the mistakes and horrors of the past, because they still affect people today.

It is in the past, and people who go on about the Empire just want to make Britain look bad. That means they don't really love Britain.

The British Empire used violence to take other people's freedom and resources for itself, and has left a legacy of inequality. We need to understand the past so we can make the right choices today.

"WAIT. Why is this even an argument?"

GREAT QUESTION.

For some people, asking questions about the rights and wrongs of the British Empire can feel like a challenge to British identity itself. For others, it is a way to understand their lives. It can be a way to challenge racism, inequality, and poverty. Understanding the facts of what happened doesn't mean your country is any less important to you. Talking about our stories and experiences helps us to work out our feelings about our past and our present. The past may be gone but it is not forgotten, is it? It affects us all, here, and now. If bad things were done by the British Empire, should they be rectified or compensated, even if it's hundreds of years later?

So many questions! And to answer them we need to understand and talk about what happened.

Luckily, you have this book!

Chapter Seventeen

The British Empire – thumbs up or thumbs down?

One of the most heated points of this debate is the morality – or otherwise – of the British Empire. Morality is the concept of doing the right thing. Take the example of slavery. As we read earlier, slavery was a huge part of the Empire; how it grew, how it became profitable, and how it traded. The wealth of many families today can be traced back to owning slaves. It wasn't just the aristocracy, ordinary people owned slaves too.

The money generated by slavery made the country wealthier and improved living standards.

Imagine your ancestors became wealthy due to the slave labour of other human beings. How would you feel about your money?

Now, imagine the opposite, that your ancestors were one of the enslaved people. How would you feel?

We are not directly responsible for these terrible things, but all of us must live with the consequences. And if the impacts of the British Empire are still with us, it means we can't pretend they don't affect us. Because we know they are real. We must feel something. But what? And if we feel something, what, if anything, should we do about it?

Was it wrong to have an empire?

Empires are about getting rich, powerful and beating your enemies. To achieve that, they steal land, kill people, burn down cities, and help themselves to other people's wealth and resources. All things we consider wrong in ordinary life. Human history has been filled with all sorts of empires and the wars between them.

It's how large groups of people were often ruled, and how the states dealt with each other. Like all empires, the British Empire did unsavoury things to get power and stay in power. So, was the British Empire really any better or worse than any other empire?

Empires like people to think that they exist for an important reason. And the British Empire was no exception. One justification was to spread Christianity. Another was a responsibility to "civilise" people who the Empire thought were inferior. This was even given a name: the "white man's burden", coined by British poet Rudyard Kipling. It suggested that the Empire was a heavy responsibility for Britain, not a benefit, because it was there to guide "primitive" people, and not to make Britain wealthy.

Science was manipulated and warped to promote the wrongheaded idea that white-skinned people were superior to brown-skinned people, who were in turn superior to black-skinned people.

The early years of the British Empire were all about getting rich, and to do that, all the rules were broken: piracy, slavery and stealing to name just a few.

In the Age of Discovery, European powers competed to see who could become the richest, often jealous of each other. They didn't just fight over borders between their own countries. They tried to carve up *other* parts of the world, not caring that people already lived there and the land belonged to them.

To keep power, rebellions and independence movements were crushed, rebels imprisoned or killed, and sometimes there were horrific consequences for entire communities and nations.

Good privateer or wicked pirate?

In 1560, Queen Elizabeth I created a military group of privateers called the Sea Dogs. She gave them a special letter called a "marque" with permission to attack Spanish ships. The loot was split between the ship owners, the captain, crew, and the government.

The privateers got rich and so did England. The plundered wealth was used to fund the very beginnings of the Empire, especially the New World colonies in Virginia, today's USA, and the Caribbean.

The most famous privateers were Sir Francis Drake, Sir John Hawkins, and Sir Walter Raleigh, who were first pirates and then became privateers, stealing goods and people and taking land for themselves. Hawkins even became England's first slave-trader in 1562. When they returned to England, they could get a high position in the Royal Court.

Now, pirates also plundered ships. But instead of giving a share to the British monarch, they traded directly with the new colonies in North America and kept all the money. Piracy was a criminal offence that could lead to the death sentence.

But what really was the difference between a privateer and a pirate?

Women at sea

Life on the ocean waves wasn't just for men. There were plenty of women who went to sea as servants, cooks, laundresses, naval officers and even pirates. The pirate, Blackbeard, thought having women on board a ship invited bad luck. That didn't seem to be the case for two famous female pirates Anne Bonny and Mary Read who lived around the turn of the 18th century.

Not everyone feels the same way

In the 19th and 20th centuries the British Empire was established. Now it needed a reason to justify its actions, and to do that it needed to create a new story and identity for itself. At that moment it was true that Britain *was* the most powerful nation on Earth. It *was* the richest country. It *did* have the most powerful navy. It *did* cross the largest landmass. Technological, scientific and medical innovations *did* happen in Britain. Britain *did* play a pivotal role in the World Wars. All of this is true.

You might hear echoes of all of this when people talk about Britain today.

Although, as is often the case with big bold headlines, this doesn't give the whole picture. A great deal of all that was due to the labour, wealth, resources, and talents of hundreds of millions of people around the world, often taken for free.

And what we also need to think about is that the Britain today is a different Britain from 200 or even 100 years ago. While the Empire is gone, the identity it created still dominates our feelings about being British.

And no wonder. It's nice to think of your country as the biggest, the most powerful, the richest AND the most moral.

Asking questions about what really happened and why, can leave some people feeling as though someone is trying to take away that identity. It can even make people angry at those who ask questions to find out what really happened, and to make sure as many different stories are told as possible. But asking questions and finding more stories: isn't that what good thinkers do?

All of this might feel hard, and it's okay for us to talk about the challenges. But talking about them is the right thing to do. In fact, it's perfectly normal. And what successful countries do all the time. National identities are always being reinvented. And the best identities are the ones that know exactly who they are and feel a mix of emotions include self-awareness and criticism, and realising where mistakes were made. If the past is something that should inform our identity, it must be all the past, not just the pride.

What should we do about it now?

In our imaginary story of the descendants of slave-owners and enslaved people (see page 202) we can see that while the British Empire itself has ended, its effects have not. People are starting to discuss what can be done about the past.

Reparations are being asked for by descendants of enslaved people. Countries whose artefacts have been stolen are asking for them to be returned. Big institutions like the National Trust are researching the history of its properties and how slavery and wealth from the Empire may have built them. Some people are simply asking for an apology. Things in the past can't be changed, but an acknowledgement of a wrong can help with the healing process.

But mostly, people just want to talk about the events of the past, so we can create an identity that is based on shared, open, honest histories that includes everyone's story.

And while the past has already been written, the *Story of Now* is something that we can write ourselves.

Chapter Eighteen

Britishness

In this final chapter in this section, we're going to think about **Britain's own idea of itself** and how our ideas of Britain and Britishness have been fundamentally shaped by the British Empire.

Each of us has an identity that changes over time. None of us are the same person we were 10 years ago. In the same way, **national identity** changes over time too.

Time for a quiz!

Let's start by finding out how much you know about some of the things that are part of Britain's national identity.

1. *What is the actual full name of the country?*

2. *When did this name get created?*

3. *So why do we call it Britain, England, Great Britain, or the United Kingdom?*

4. *When was the national anthem first sung?*

5. *Which of these early groups of immigrants to Britain is the odd one out? Angles, Saxons, Jutes, Frisians, Celts, Romans, Britishers, Vikings, Picts, Gaels and Norse.*

6. *Who is the first person we have evidence lived in Britain?*

7. *What's the British flag called?*

You're clever enough to work out that there's a reason I put all those questions together (apart from it's cool to know facts). They highlight there's no one single thing called Britishness and no single definition of a British person. These are constantly changing.

Building a British story

When Queen Elizabeth I's privateers first set sail to gather the riches of the world, the kind of Britishness we think about today didn't even exist. England was a small country, with few friends, a ramshackle navy and quite poor. Its goal was to trade and make money (and if it had to plunder or kill, so be it).

The piracy, slave-trading, disease-bringing, gun-toting, opium-smuggling antics are probably far from the stereotypes commonly held of the British at the height of the Empire. In fact, we don't usually talk about that kind of Britishness at all.

We tell the stories of people like Sir John Hawkins and Walter Raleigh as pioneers and heroes, who discovered new lands and brought wealth to Britain. You can see immediately how these different perspectives lead to different ideas about what it means to be British.

Which bits of the story do we choose to tell?

Today, when we think of being British, we might think of people playing cricket on a green lawn, or tea served by a butler on a table with a white cloth. There are the ideas of fair play and stiff upper lip or ensuring you always queue!

As we've journeyed together through this book, how have your ideas developed? Are these the images you still have or want to have?

Fitting in or standing apart?

When the British first arrived in India they wore Indian clothes, learnt local languages, and even married Indian women and had families with children described as Anglo-Indian (their descendants still exist today). They even had their own description, the White Mughals. Britishness was confident and was happy to embrace lots of cultures.

As Britain increased its power over India, it became important that British identity was kept very distinct from Indian identity. British men were forbidden from marrying Indian women.

A desire to dominate

Even though England had had a weak, ramshackle navy, the British Empire turned itself into a nation with dominating seafaring technology. It had steamships, a merchant navy, and sailors from around the world. Its identity went from an aspiration, "Britannia, rule the waves!" to a declaration of power "Britannia rules the waves!" (See how much difference a comma can make?)

The "man on the ground"

There are lots of British Empire stories of men who established British power around the world. But these "men on the ground" also did some horrible things. How should we remember these men? Should it be about the good things, or the bad things, or both? How does that shape the idea of Britishness today?

Cecil Rhodes and the birth of Apartheid

The "man on the ground" in southern Africa was Cecil Rhodes (1853–1902) and he was so important, they named a country after him – Rhodesia. Today Rhodesia is gone, now part of Zimbabwe and Zambia. Rhodes led the British expansion across southern Africa and believed in the inferiority of Africans. His ideas and attitudes would become the basis of apartheid. Apartheid is the Afrikaans word for "separateness" or "being apart". Apartheid law began in South Africa in 1948 and enforced the separation of whites from blacks and other non-white groups. It was a legal and physical form of racism supported by the courts. It was illegal for black children and adults to use buses, park benches, public toilets, hotels, or any other service if it had a sign saying "Whites Only". Apartheid only ended in 1994.

Is it okay to disagree?

There was plenty of disagreement during the Empire itself about its actions and behaviours, and if Britain should even have an Empire or not. Should the idea of disagreement be part of Britishness? And if so, how do we reflect our own disagreement about the rights and wrongs of the British Empire today?

A "civilising mission"

At the height of its power in the late Victorian era the British Empire needed a new idea of Britishness. Britain was described as the "workshop of the world". It wanted to justify its rule over all the colonies. And as the 19th century progressed, it also had to find ways to keep the workforce at home quiet, too. Those who had power wanted to keep it, and didn't want to give it away to people who were fighting for rights. These movements for social change included fighting for workers' rights (though the labour movement) and for universal suffrage (the right for women and working men to vote). You can read more about these movements on page 114.

So, the ideas of British superiority and the civilising mission started to build. It's one of the reasons why in this period so many of the statues, stories and public spaces were created to assert the greatness of the Empire. Remember Edward Colston's statue in 1895, but who lived more than 150 years earlier?

This way the violent actions and the rule of the British Empire could be justified. And the superiority was claimed in every aspect: the colour of skin, political systems, military power, language, literature, technology and so on.

You read earlier about how science was used to say some kinds of people were superior to others (see page 203). Today, this idea has been abandoned as lacking scientific validity, and instead is seen as a social idea used by empires to justify treating non-white people differently.

Unfortunately missionaries were used in a similar way to spread the religion of Christianity. It was a way of erasing native religions and customs, and passing on language and ideas and that were more in line with beliefs held by the Empire.

This makes sense, because if you want to rule over other people, make them work for you for next to nothing AND you want to take their resources, you must find a way to justify it.

Nowhere was the civilising mission considered more important than when talking about the rights of colonised women. From 1883 to 1907 Lord Cromer was the British Consul, which ruled over Egypt, where a large proportion of the population is Muslim. He claimed he was making life better for Egyptian women by forcing them to remove their headscarves. But when he came back to the UK in 1910, he founded an organisation to *oppose* the women's suffrage movement which was campaigning for women to have the right to vote.

Thankfully, today we believe in the equality of all human beings.

English language and literature

Most people like to think of the language and literary heritage that they are part of as the best or most beautiful, and the British are no different. Spreading the English language across the world was therefore seen as a gift bestowed upon the colonial subjects. But across the British Empire, the people there already had long sophisticated literary heritages such as the libraries of Mali, the Islamic texts of Arabia which triggered the European Renaissance, to the Sanskrit scriptures of India, and many more.

Even in Britain, regional dialects, and accents were looked down on. But really, forcing people to speak English was just a way to ensure the British rulers could communicate and enforce their orders. And making "proper" English (referred to as King's or Queen's English) as the only way to have influence, authority and power kept class hierarchies in place. And in the process, all the local languages, regional dialects and cultures were made to seem inferior, and some were lost forever, because people stopped speaking them.

A plucky little island

One of the most powerful stories of Britishness comes from being on the winning side in the two World Wars. But did Britain really win all by itself?

Did you know:

In World War I

- Over 2.5 million men from around the British Empire fought for Britain, including 1.4 million from the Indian subcontinent. Soldiers also came from Canada, Australia, New Zealand, South Africa, and Rhodesia (part of today's Zimbabwe and Zambia).

- The West Indian colonies contributed nearly £2 million from tax revenues and donations for war supplies such as planes and ambulances.

- Between 116,000 and 350,000 soldiers who were killed in World War 1 from African, Indian or Egyptian origin were not commemorated by name. A report by the Commonwealth Commission determined that this was due to racist views against them.

In World War II

- 2.5 million soldiers from the Indian subcontinent fought for the UK.

- The colonies contributed £23.3 million in gifts, £10.7 million in interest-free loans and £14 million low-interest loans, even though in most colonies people lived in poverty with few schools and hospitals.

 Black and Indian soldiers were not allowed to be officers or serve in the same regiment as white British soldiers. They were also paid less. It was considered improper for them to be in charge. But perfectly proper for them to die for Britain.

Creating a place called home

Today, some people are told that they are not British because they are born somewhere else or have a different religion or skin colour, or they aren't as important because they are working class, poor or live outside London. What often follows is a horrible discussion about who is more British, who has more rights and who should be grateful. All of this is hurtful, and it damages everyone in the country.

What would be really powerful would be to create a sense of Britishness that celebrates this amazing country we have built, and that belongs to everyone.

The Windrush Generation

After the two World Wars, Britain had run out of money and didn't have enough people to rebuild the country, and so it invited people from its colonies with the promise of employment and better lives.

In 1948 the government made a law saying that all Commonwealth citizens could have British passports and work in Britain. At this invitation, people migrated from the West Indies, India and Pakistan and Cyprus. In 1948, a group came from the Caribbean on a ship called the Empire Windrush (see *photo section*). Today, British Caribbean people who came to the United Kingdom between 1948 and 1971 are called the Windrush Generation.

However, in the 2010s the Windrush scandal happened. Tens of thousands of people from the Windrush Generation were told that, after over 60 years of living and working in Britain, they were actually NOT British after all. Some were deported to live in countries they barely knew, or had never lived in. They were told Britain was not their home, even though they'd lived in Britain their whole lives.

In 2018 the UK government apologised for their appalling treatment of the Windrush Generation.

A shared sense of Britishness

Having a shared sense of national identity is an important part of a successful country, for making everyone feel like they belong (and that feeling is important). And that means that individuals within the country are more likely to be successful too.

That's why learning as many different stories and perspectives as possible, as we've been doing in this book, is so important. So that you can have beautiful conversations with people and understand each other better.

Thinking about *all the things* that contributed to Britishness

Some things are often discussed about Britishness: democracy, rule of law, freedom, modernity, wealth, religion, civilisation, technology, innovation, entrepreneurship, the English language and British culture.

But there's lots of other things we've learnt about in this book too: different kinds of people, religions, cultures and languages; the nations in the UK that contributed, the parts of each country who worked so hard and gave so much.

Deciding what is or isn't British affects people's sense of belonging. It also affects whether they feel at home here or not. Anyone who lives here, or who has ever lived in a part of the British Empire, has a share in the British story and in its future, including you. Everyone who was ever a part of this once vast empire are all a part of this story.

Building "Brand Britain"

Nation-branding gives a country an identity so people can feel good about living there. It also creates trade and tourism from other countries around the world.

Can you design a look and feel for "Brand Britain"? Think about what words might describe the kind of Britain that you would like to build.

Your successful brand should understand your own history, strengths and challenges, but you also must understand *other people's ideas of you* and pull them together to represent *your idea of what you want to be*.

What words and images would people in Britain use to describe the country? This might vary depending on how old they are or which part of the country they live in.

What ideas do people who live in other countries have about Britain? Think about Britain's history. How might a person living in a former colony feel about Britain?

The world is changing and if Brand Britain wants to be part of it, it needs to change too. What do you think Britain needs to become to ensure its success?

What do you think a logo would look like – what image, colours and shapes?

Based on all the above, can you create one line that summarises Brand Britain?

So, what exactly *does* it mean to be British?

It's a question that has puzzled all sorts of people, from ordinary people like you and me, to social scientists, politicians, businesspeople, global leaders, educators, thinkers, philosophers, historians and many more.

It doesn't seem to have one fixed answer. We have changing ideas about ourselves. Even the idea of Britishness and the things we associate with being British change all the time.

It's an interesting question, but in the meantime it's useful to ask *practical questions* about the country today. Questions that will make a difference to our lives, and build a thriving country that helps every individual including me and you to have the best chance of success.

What do we want all the people who live here to feel? What do we want to stand for as a country and how do we want to behave when it comes to other countries? Most important of all, what kind of country does Britain want to be in the future?

The story starts now.

Part Four

What's next?

Chapter Nineteen

Dear reader, it's your turn

We've been on a huge adventure in this book, what with pirates, corporations with armies, stealing saplings to make new medicines, mining gold, building railways, migrating around the world, and reshaping entire natural habitats. The centuries of the world's biggest empire have been a roller coaster ride of morality and historical discovery, leading to some important but also challenging thinking about who and what we are today, and what kind of shared future we want to live in together. But, as they say, nothing good was ever easy!

What have you learnt that you didn't know before? I must admit there were lots of new things I discovered as I researched and wrote this book. Some filled me with awe, like how the invention of the telegraph transformed communications as we know it and laid the foundations for our digital world today. Some broke my heart, like the stories of the home children who were sent to the colonies for better lives, but never saw their families again, and were made to feel ashamed for who they were. I cry every time I think about the horrors of slavery. Some felt very raw to me, like the famines that were made worse in India by British policies and the suppression of rebellions in East Africa; both are places connected to my family history. The stories of children that suffered lifelong and even fatal consequences in the Industrial Revolution were also very painful, because my own children are those young ages.

Perhaps most eye-opening for me were the sheer number of different stories and experiences, each of which gave me a new insight into how the British Empire affected all sorts of people. One of the most difficult things for me was that I couldn't include more of them. (My editor said, "Shelina, we know you love stories, but we are running out of space... No. More. Stories.)

That's where you come in. You can add stories that you've been inspired to learn more about. You too can investigate, discuss and research more stories. They might be to do with the British Empire, or other local and national histories that have affected you. Perhaps, like me, you might find that the most important one is yours: your family's, that of the place you live and those of the people around you like the stories of your friends, teachers, and neighbours.

The more stories we know, and the better we tell and share those stories, the better people we become. So, if there's one thing – just one thing – that you take away from this book, I'd like it to be the importance of hearing as many kinds of stories as possible, especially knowing your own.

Time to start the conversation (over a cuppa and a biscuit)

We talked earlier about the heated debate that surrounds discussions of the British Empire. And that is usually because we are talking "at" each other rather than having a conversation. Conversations allow us to understand each other and to understand each other's experiences now and our hopes for the future, and we don't always have to agree about everything. To have productive, joyful, meaningful conversations, we need to have shared information about the past and we need to know how our own stories fit in. That's why this whole book has been about understanding the British Empire together, and why often I've posed questions rather than give you answers. Because it isn't for me to tell you what to think. It's for you to **decide for yourself**. So now you have begun to understand the British Empire, it's time to start a conversation. It's time to discover your own story.

Our future history

At the very beginning of the book (see page 25), we imagined children like you who lived a hundred years ago, and what they would have been taught – and *not* taught – about the British Empire at the very moment when it was at its largest and most powerful. I wonder if they could have imagined how things would change for the British Empire over the coming century?

Now you're here and it's your turn. What stories about your life would *you* tell kids in a hundred years from now? What would you like them to know about you? What would you like their world to be like? What kind of future country should Britain be and what role should it play in the world? If you're living in a country once colonised by Britain, what would you like your country to be like?

You now have the opportunity to learn from our past, add your own story into it, and think about how you can help to make a bright and exciting future for everyone.

History isn't far away or dead. History is our story, the story of who we are now.

Your job, your very extremely important job, is to **build our future history** and write the next chapter in this book.

Ready?

Chapter Twenty

Let's discover your story

Investigating your own story is exciting! But where do you start? Here are some helpful ways to begin.

You might be interested in finding out about your own family, or perhaps you want to work with a friend to investigate theirs. Maybe you've always been intrigued by a building, park or place you walk past regularly. Maybe it's the local library, school, or community centre where you picked up this book!

Talking to other people

The people around us are treasure troves of stories. Sometimes their stories are even more riveting than the stories we read in books because they are the most important stories of all to our own lives. Oral stories – which are the ones ordinary people tell – are precious because they are so rarely captured.

By asking someone about their story and writing it down, you are doing something incredibly powerful. **YOU are making history**. And at the same time, you are finding out about who YOU are and are taking charge of YOUR OWN STORY.

People love to tell their stories, and realise that their own lives were part of a big historical change. But it can be hard to know where to start. Here are some ideas of questions you can ask.

- When and where were you born? What were the names of your parents? What do you remember about them? What are your earliest memories?

- If you went to school, what was it like? What subjects did you study and like? What do you remember about what was happening in the world while you were at school?

Can you tell me about two or three big national or international events that affected your life? What do you remember about them, what were people talking about at the time, and how did it affect you? These might include things like wars, national independence, change of laws, new people moving into the area or their own migration.

Did you or anyone in your family migrate – perhaps from one part of the country to another, or from one country to another? Why? What was it like to move and how did it feel when you got there?

How to be a super sleuth!

Do you think you could be the Sherlock Holmes of your own story? Ask the oldest person you know about the name and date of birth of the oldest family member that they remember.

If that person was born in the UK, you can visit your library and find their birth certificate and marriage information and, depending on how old they are, their parents may appear on a public census. Every ten years the government conducts a census which records the details of every person living in Britain. It is important to know who is living in your country because it helps you to work out how many people are needed to support your population, like how many police, doctors, or teachers you need to train. The latest census took place in 2021.

Censuses have been made every ten years since 1841. These are made public once 100 years has passed. So, if you are looking for a person who lived over 100 years ago, you can use the census to uncover fascinating information about where they lived, what jobs they did and how many people lived in their house. Once you have found your family member, you can find out who their parents were, when they were born and where they lived. This way, you can track your ancestors one generation at a time – who they were, what they did, where they lived – and you can piece together a story.

If you don't have ancestors in the UK, you can also use the census to discover the history of a building. Is your house over 100 years old? What are the stories of the people who lived there before you?

Perhaps your family has their history in another country. Ask your family members if they have any old passports, birth certificates and photographs. You can then explore the areas where people lived and events that happened that might have impacted them.

There are also online tools and services to help explore further but please do make sure you ask an adult for support to stay safe (and it is also a sneaky way to help *them* to work out their own story too. Grown-ups need to do the same!).

Where are you really from?

A lot of people ask me, "Where are you from?", and I say, "London!"

But there's often a follow up question, "No, but where are you really from?", as though the person asking doesn't believe I could – or should – be from London, or in fact Britain. I know why. It's because I have brown skin. Sadly, a lot of other people face this too. It's what we were talking about earlier (see page 220), about who is considered British.

It's absolutely fine to ask someone where they are from, but once they answer, just smile, and accept it. After all, they really do know where they are from!

Places have stories too

Sometimes local names can be a clue to an interesting story. Many towns and villages will even have local histories written and perhaps even published about them. A building or place might have its own history recorded on its website.

When you're walking past a statue or monument, stop and read the plaque which might have dates or people's names which you can then investigate in more detail. Building dates can be great hints about what might have happened and why.

Try searching through local newspaper archives to find out more. Local libraries can be excellent places to discover local history and have online tools to help. There might even be local history societies! Maybe you could set one up if there isn't!

Pick a topic from this book

Right at the beginning, I did say that this book couldn't cover everything from the whole of the British Empire. And that's why YOU are such an important part of our collective future history. Each of us has different interests and things that make us curious. As you think about what you're learnt in this book, and from the people and places around us, what do you want to know more about? It might be a topic from the British Empire. Or maybe it's about another empire or period of history that affected your family. Maybe you can use the tips above for more research. Maybe you can turn it into a family or school project to find out more?

Maybe, just maybe, you could even write your own book about it!

A history of the British Empire

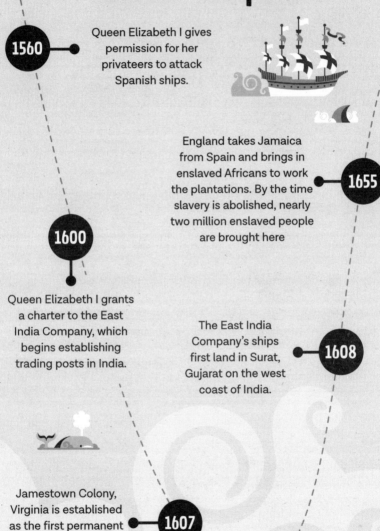

1560
Queen Elizabeth I gives permission for her privateers to attack Spanish ships.

1655
England takes Jamaica from Spain and brings in enslaved Africans to work the plantations. By the time slavery is abolished, nearly two million enslaved people are brought here

1600
Queen Elizabeth I grants a charter to the East India Company, which begins establishing trading posts in India.

1608
The East India Company's ships first land in Surat, Gujarat on the west coast of India.

1607
Jamestown Colony, Virginia is established as the first permanent English settlement on the American continent.

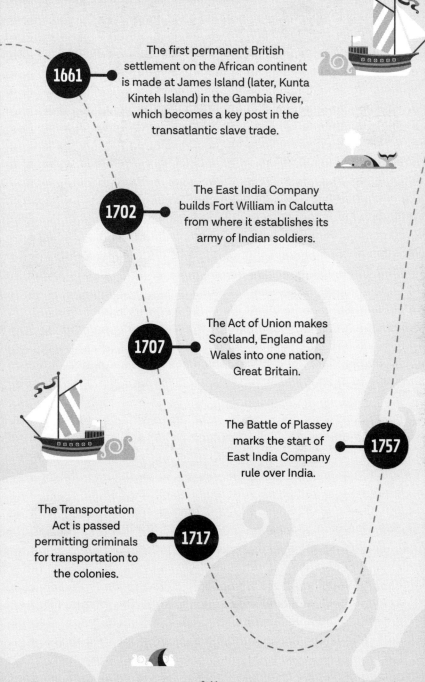

1661
The first permanent British settlement on the African continent is made at James Island (later, Kunta Kinteh Island) in the Gambia River, which becomes a key post in the transatlantic slave trade.

1702
The East India Company builds Fort William in Calcutta from where it establishes its army of Indian soldiers.

1707
The Act of Union makes Scotland, England and Wales into one nation, Great Britain.

1757
The Battle of Plassey marks the start of East India Company rule over India.

1717
The Transportation Act is passed permitting criminals for transportation to the colonies.

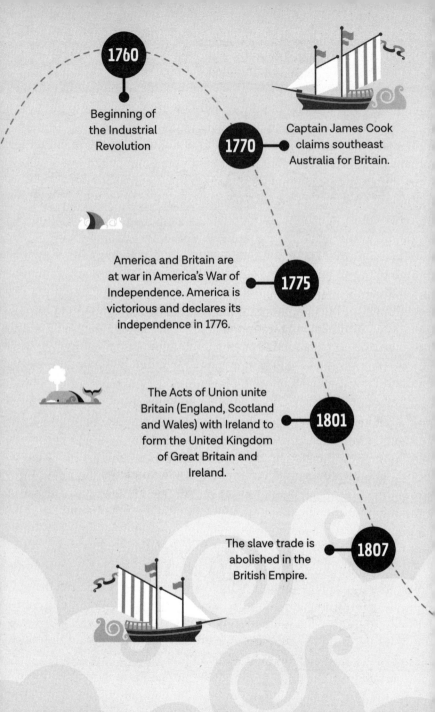

1760

Beginning of the Industrial Revolution

1770

Captain James Cook claims southeast Australia for Britain.

1775

America and Britain are at war in America's War of Independence. America is victorious and declares its independence in 1776.

1801

The Acts of Union unite Britain (England, Scotland and Wales) with Ireland to form the United Kingdom of Great Britain and Ireland.

1807

The slave trade is abolished in the British Empire.

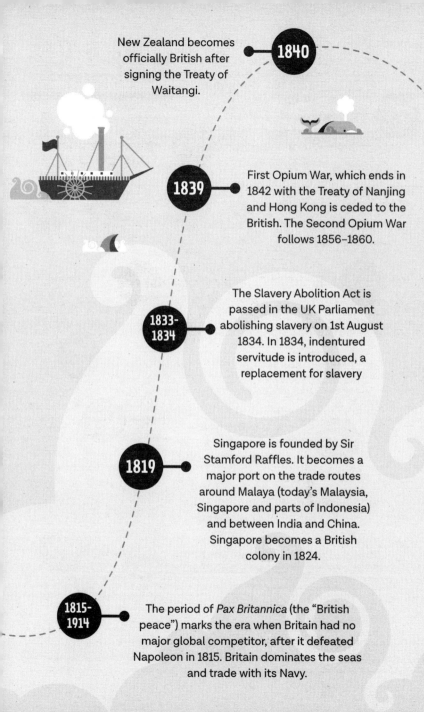

New Zealand becomes officially British after signing the Treaty of Waitangi.

1840

1839 First Opium War, which ends in 1842 with the Treaty of Nanjing and Hong Kong is ceded to the British. The Second Opium War follows 1856–1860.

1833–1834 The Slavery Abolition Act is passed in the UK Parliament abolishing slavery on 1st August 1834. In 1834, indentured servitude is introduced, a replacement for slavery

1819 Singapore is founded by Sir Stamford Raffles. It becomes a major port on the trade routes around Malaya (today's Malaysia, Singapore and parts of Indonesia) and between India and China. Singapore becomes a British colony in 1824.

1815–1914 The period of *Pax Britannica* (the "British peace") marks the era when Britain had no major global competitor, after it defeated Napoleon in 1815. Britain dominates the seas and trade with its Navy.

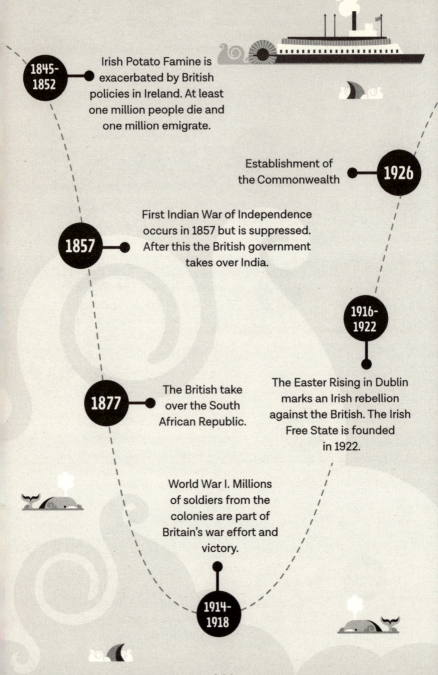

1845-1852
Irish Potato Famine is exacerbated by British policies in Ireland. At least one million people die and one million emigrate.

1926
Establishment of the Commonwealth

1857
First Indian War of Independence occurs in 1857 but is suppressed. After this the British government takes over India.

1916-1922

1877
The British take over the South African Republic.

The Easter Rising in Dublin marks an Irish rebellion against the British. The Irish Free State is founded in 1922.

World War I. Millions of soldiers from the colonies are part of Britain's war effort and victory.

1914-1918

244

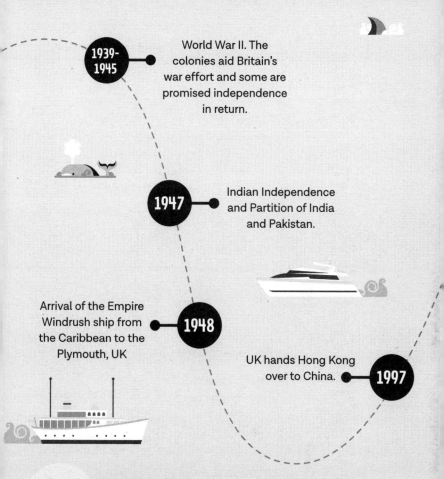

1939-1945 World War II. The colonies aid Britain's war effort and some are promised independence in return.

1947 Indian Independence and Partition of India and Pakistan.

1948 Arrival of the Empire Windrush ship from the Caribbean to the Plymouth, UK

1997 UK hands Hong Kong over to China.

What's happening now?

The effects of the British Empire are still felt by countries and people today. The UK's taxpayers finally paid off the cost of the compensation given to slave owners, totalling £17 billion in today's money. Scotland had a referendum in 2014 to vote for independence. Although it wasn't passed, many people still want the country to be independent. Countries around the world that still have King Charles III as their head of state are thinking of becoming republics. These include Jamaica and Australia. Barbados decided it would become a republic in 2021.

The "Pink Map" of the British Empire c. 1920s

This map was known as the "pink map" and it shows the territories of the British Empire as it would have looked in the 1920s. This is when the Empire was at the height of its power. Clearly in this book it's not pink (sorry, it's a black-and-white book). But remember we talked about children, like you, living a hundred years ago? Well, this is the map that might have hung on their classroom walls.

In this map, north faces up and Greenwich is centred. This makes places further from the equator look bigger. So, Africa should really be 125 times bigger than Britain and twice as large as Canada. Britain wanted to look much bigger than it really was, to appear to be at the centre of the world, and show off its vast, well-connected territories. This is excellent for projecting world domination!

Glossary

Aboriginal Australian - the various First Nations people of the Australian mainland and many of its islands

Age of Discovery - a period from the 15th century to the 17th century, during which seafaring Europeans explored, colonised and conquered regions across the globe

Annex (a country) – when a country takes by force a part of a country or a territory belonging to another country

Backstory – the story behind an event

Bankrupt – when a country or person does not have enough money to pay their debts

Boudicca - a queen of the Iceni, who led a revolt against Roman rule in Britain

Boycott – an act of protest by refusing to buy, use, or participate in something

Brand (on to skin) - an identifying mark burned on livestock, criminals or enslaved people with a branding iron

Brand (product) - a product manufactured by a particular company under a particular name

British Raj - the direct British rule over areas of India that had been conquered by Britain, also known as British India

Capital (money) – wealth in the form of money or valuable goods

Chattel slavery - the act of enslaving and owning of human beings and their children as property, able to be bought, sold, and forced to work without wages

Colony - a country or area that is under the control of another country

Commodity - a raw material or primary agricultural product that can be bought and sold, such as tea or cotton

Commodity-dependent – when a country only grows one type of crop, such as tea, so its fortunes are tied to how valuable that crop is to the global market and is not protected if the crop harvest fails

Commonwealth - an international association consisting of the UK together with states that were previously part of the British Empire, and dependencies.

Compensation - something, typically money, awarded to someone in recognition of loss, suffering, or injury

Concession - a thing that is granted, especially in response to demands

Corporate imperialism - when a specific company become so powerful in another nation that they can influence the policy of those nations' governments

Corporation - a large company or group of companies authorised to act as a single entity

Cryptocurrency - a digital currency in which transactions are verified and records maintained by a decentralised system rather than by a country.

Decolonisation - the action of a country withdrawing from a former colony, leaving it independent

Dynasty - a succession of people from the same family, often used to describe a line of monarchs or emperors

East India Company - East India Company was an English company formed to trade with the East Indies and East Asia.

Exploitation - the action of treating someone unfairly in order to benefit from their work

Freedom of Movement – the right to travel from place to place
Freetown – a city in Sierra Leone, founded as a home for freed slaves

Guild - a medieval association of craftsmen or merchants

Hierarchy - a system in which members of a society are ranked according to their status or race

Indentured labour - a form of labour in which a person is contracted to work for a specific number of years
Industrial Revolution – the process when the country moved from a handmade or agricultural economy to one dominated by industry and mass-produced goods

Legacy – an effect that exists today that has come from the past

Methodist – a branch of the Christian Protestant faith
Middle classes - the social group between the upper and working classes, often made up of business people and their families
Mint – a place where coins are made
Missionary - a person sent on a religious mission, especially one sent to promote Christianity in a foreign country
Monopoly – when there is no competing manufacturer for a product so a single company has control over the price and distribution of that product to that market
Mutiny - an rebellion against the proper authorities

Opium - a reddish-brown heavy-scented addictive and deadly drug, prepared from the juice of the opium poppy

Piecener - someone (often a child) who worked in a cotton mill and whose job it was to join broken threads together

Quaker - a Christian movement founded by George Fox around 1650 and devoted to peaceful principles

Rupee - the unit of money of India, Pakistan, Sri Lanka, Nepal, Mauritius, and the Seychelles

Social mobility – the movement of people from one social class to another
Smallpox – a deadly infection caused by the variola virus, that was wiped out following a vaccination programme
State - a nation or territory under one government

Telegraph - a system for transmitting messages across great distances along a wire
Textiles – cloth or woven fabric
Trade union - an organized association of workers in a trade, group of trades, or profession, formed to protect their rights
Transportation – the practice of transporting convicts to a colony to live

Upper class – a very small group of people at the top of the social hierarchy, consisting of the aristocracy and wealthy landowners

Working classes - the social group at the bottom of the social heirarchy that consists of people who usually do more physical types of work

Index

A note from the author

There's a tightly knit band of amazing people without whom this book would not be what it is. My talented, visionary and patient editor Gemma Farr who has been a dream, and the best editorial partner I could have asked for; the creative and inspirational art director Matt Drew; my agent Hannah Weatherill whose belief and brilliance gave me wings; the book's illustrator Laura Greenan who can create magic, power and goosebumps from her art; and a special thank you to Jane Harris for making it happen, and whose talent and passion are a joy to behold, and which through this book and others I hope will change the world.

Thank you to these special people for giving me absolutely vital advice, guidance and life-affirming support (not to mention the mending of heartbreak and the re-igniting of the fires when it all got a bit much). I also thank them for their solidarity and encouragement in ensuring this book and its messages came to life: Lubaaba Al Azami, Shaheen Bilgrami, Roohi Hasan, Elaine Heaver, Michael Mumisa, Marcus Ryder and David Veevers. And the biggest shout out to the ones who have been my absolute rocks when I needed them most: Hajera Memon, Siddika Dhalla and Mr Shelina.

Finally, a special mention for my special girls, who are the entirety of my heart, for whom the book was written, who helped me write it and make sure it's just right for kids like them: Hana and Iman. I love you, you are amazing and you inspire me every day. (Also, please tidy your rooms, thank you). Over to you to write our future history.